DIFFERENCE
Maker

Volume 5

DARE TO BE A

DIFFERENCE
Maker
Volume 5

DIFFERENCE MAKERS WHO DARE TO LIVE
WITH PASSION, FOLLOW THEIR PURPOSE
AND COMMIT TO HELPING OTHERS!

MICHELLE PRINCE

Dedication

To all the "Difference Makers" in the world
who are making a difference by following your heart.
Thanks for letting your "light" shine!

Introduction

For many years as I worked in "Corporate America" I would say to myself, "I just want to make a difference!" I was selling software and I'm sure I was making some difference for my clients but not in the way I wanted to. I wanted to help, serve, encourage and motivate people. I wanted to make a positive impact on their lives but I didn't know how...how could just one person really make a significant difference? So I didn't...for a long time. I continued to work in an area that wasn't my passion or calling. I didn't follow my heart and God's promptings to go in the direction of my purpose and dreams. Instead, I just let year after year go by feeling unfulfilled, unhappy, and spiritually broken.

That is, until one day in 2008 when I had my "aha" moment. It hit me like a ton of bricks that it's my responsibility to follow my passions and purpose. No one can do that for me. I took action to write my first book, *Winning In Life Now*, began to speak, motivate and mentor others to live their best life and, as they say, "the rest is history."

What I found over this journey is that we all have a desire to make a difference. We all want to live with passion and follow our God-given callings; our purpose. It's through this understanding that I decided to write this series of books.

Dare To Be A Difference Maker 5 is my vision to have a unique collection of narratives, not only from inspired leaders, but also from those I see making a difference and impacting others in their everyday personal and professional life. These stories are about *real* people who are making a *real* difference, even on a small scale.

My mission in creating the "Difference Maker Movement" and in writing the series of *Dare To Be A Difference Maker* books is that you will gain inspiration, wisdom, and the courage you need in order to get through life's tough challenges and make a difference for others in the process.

So many people I speak with these days discuss their issues as though they are losing hope. It is my vision for this book to reach the masses and have a powerful effect on people in their everyday lives. It is my prayer that this book, and all the volumes, will breathe new life into your mind and spirit and that it will inspire you to take action in order to help others.

I've selected an exclusive group of difference-makers who I know can motivate, inspire, and be a part of a movement to change people's lives. Everyone can do this; it just takes commitment and honoring of our unique and sacred gifts. It is to those people I dedicate this book.

From one "Difference Maker" to another,

Michelle

P.S. Do you or anyone you know have a story about making a difference? We are currently interviewing authors for our next book and would love to have you join us in this amazing journey. To submit an entry, please contact Info@PrincePerformance.com for more details. While one powerful story can be fascinating many can move mountains!

Table of Contents

The Fight Is On
Charles Beauford

Bodies collide suddenly with the force of a head-to-head car crash. The crowd roars, coaches scream, while you roll on the ground in pain. You've been hit hard, really hard. It's excruciating, almost too much to bear. Your opponent stands over you suspecting, hoping, wishing that was the hit or the blow that would take you out. Despite the noise of the crowd and the agony you feel, there is silence. Not literal silence, just the kind where everything else is tuned out and all you hear is your own thoughts. "Get up, get up, get up NOW! You have to get up!" I remember so vividly that third-down play where I broke my leg playing collegiate football. That was one of many opportunities I chose to do just that…get up! I went back to the huddle to prepare for the next play. This was my life. Well, in actuality, I believe this is all of our lives—at least in some respect.

I was born in 1979 at a small hospital in Xenia, Ohio. My mother and father were overjoyed because I was their first born. From the time of my birth to somewhere before my second birthday, my parents parted ways. My mom's brother, Victor, had moved to Texas a few years prior in search of greater opportunities and a better quality of life than what our small town had to offer in Ohio. My mother decided to follow my uncle Victor's leading and, since my parents were never married, it made my and my mother's transition from Ohio to Texas a little easier in some respects.

I remember the anxiety of being five years old and entering kinder-garten. Like most children, it was a big transition for me and I cried every day because I didn't want my mother to leave. Things improved, but after a few months passed, my teacher approached my mother insisting that I needed to be placed into a special needs class because of a perceived speech impediment. The teacher noticed that every time I spoke in class, I stammered and stuttered uncontrollably. My mother adamantly reject-ed any notion that I had any type of speech impediment or learning disability. I understand now that what I had was fear and insecurity that surfaced due to a lack of affirmation and confidence because of the ab-sence of a present and loving earthly father.

Many of us have struggled with fear and insecurity in certain areas of our lives because of something we lacked in our childhood. What I have learned and am learning is that the sum total of my life will never be de-termined by something I don't have. Any success that I have found has been by discovering and using the unique gifts and abilities given to me by God to serve others. As I have progressively practiced gift discovery, my life becomes more full and satisfying. At a young age I was speech deficient, but my mother fought for me to stay out of the special needs program and encouraged me to speak up and not be afraid. Through my experiences, I've learned that deficiencies are not definers, but directors that lead us into our destiny if we simply follow the clues.

By the time I was seven years old, my mother married my step-fa-ther and I inherited three siblings; two sisters and a brother. Soon after, we welcomed my baby sister into the world. We were a family of mea-ger means and lived in a three-bedroom apartment in the southwest part of Houston. My mother worked full-time and my step-father was a disabled Vietnam veteran. This was his second marriage, so my oldest step-brother and step-sister were already teenagers and had their own lives and friends to keep them occupied. My step-sister, Mona, was my closest sibling because we were only two years apart. I have vivid mem-ories of us playing inside our apartment and having a great time. We didn't get the opportunity to play outside very much because we lived in a high crime area. Aside from my play time with Mona, I felt alone, despite our full house. My step-father struggled with drug addiction for years until I was in high school. He was in and out of the home for extended periods of time and this caused a lot of tension and uncertainty in me as I matured. However, in spite of this, God always manages to bring us exactly what we need, when we need it and in the exact way we need it. Let me explain.

I met my best friend of 24 years in that apartment complex at the age of 11. He and his family lived five doors down from us. His dad was a pastor of a small church outside of Houston. They always invited me to church and took me to numerous church camps. Even though they had seven kids of their own, they always made room for me. I'm grateful for the positive influence they had in my life. After several years, my mother and I began to attend a church in the neighborhood. It was at that church that I found my true identity.

By the age of 13, I had felt the sting of disappointment from both my biological and step-fathers. I knew there had to be something more to life than what I was experiencing. It was at that time that I came into a relationship with my Heavenly Father. I knew that if anyone else failed me, at least I knew that He was with me. He was my Creator or, as I like to call Him, the Master Manufacturer. In the same way I relied on the manufacturer of a toy's instruction and the identification of something it created, I would begin to look to God for my identity, worth, and potential. After all, it was He who had provided detailed instructions on how I could operate at maximum capacity in the life I was given. So I've learned a great truth over time. It's not what you know, how much you have, but Who you have that is the key to your destiny. Since I became confident that Master Manufacturer was with me, all things now became possible.

I began to live out all these possibilities in my own life, even though I didn't fully understand my gifts and abilities at that time. However, the fact that my identity was now intact served as the foundation for my future to be built on.

Two Important Conversations

As a sophomore in high school, I was a second year starter on the varsity football team. At the age of 15, I remember being in love with going to weekly Bible studies and sharing my thoughts on the discussion topics. In the same way my body was growing rapidly from the insane amount of calories I consumed daily, my heart was growing in its desire to learn more and be more for God. One fateful night after a midweek Bible Study, I sat inside of my pastor's car and announced I was called to the ministry. Yes....you heard me right. I told the seasoned pastor of our congregation that I was called to preach. He looked at me sternly and said, "Yes, son, I believe you are." I preached my first message a few weeks before my 16th birthday in front of a crowd of around 1500 people. Keep in mind that this is the same boy who 10 years earlier could barely speak. Remember that our deficiencies are not our definers but oftentimes they are our directors to our destiny. What a joy! What an emotional high and sense of satisfaction and accomplishment! All of this would soon be turned upside down by the second important conversation.

My mother sat me down at home by the fireplace in our modest home and wanted to talk. This conversation would confirm my worst suspicions and change my approach to life forever. With all love and sincerity in her eyes, she grabbed my hand and said, "Son, I love you, but Momma don't have enough money to send you to college... so you're going to have to do well." Soon after, she asked me if I understood what she meant. Of course, I did. I responded, "Yes, Ma'am," letting her know I knew what she meant. Of course, I knew I wasn't like the other privileged kids that went to my private catholic college preparatory school.

My mom didn't have the money that my peers' parents did and I knew I had to excel. Most of the kids at my high school drove cars that would put the average working man to shame. I often caught the city bus to school, and, if not, I walked four miles one way to get there. I was able to attend this notable high school because I was a yearly scholarship recipient who worked 100 hours of community service each semester. Everyone who graduated from my high school went to excellent universities because their parents could afford to send them, regardless of their performance. When my mother and I had this conversation, it felt like I was rolling around on the ground in pain after a vicious blow. What was I to do? I went to my room and pondered her words all night. By the next morning, I decided to take her advice and "Just Do Well!"

From that day forward, my work ethic and commitment to excel exploded. At that moment, without realizing it, I embraced the necessity of personal excellence to succeed in life. I went on to receive multiple scholarship offers for academics and athletics. I accepted an athletic scholarship to the University of Houston where I started four years and was a team captain.

During my time in college I was blessed to be a part of and lead an athletic Bible study on campus for four years. The entire premise of the group was 1001 ways to illustrate the necessity of the Great Manufacturer in our lives in order to achieve peak performance on and off the field of play. Our group often joined with other groups on campus that were like-minded. We even had discussions with groups that believed there were several great manufacturers and others who didn't believe there was a Great Manufacturer at all. With all the highs of my college experience came some definite losses. The church mentioned earlier completely fell apart, based on some decisions made by the leaders. All of a sudden, I had nowhere to go to church, nowhere to learn and grow.

After a few years in college, my step-brother who I grew up with died, and that was a tough time for my entire family. Not to mention the coach who recruited me to the university was abruptly fired. To add insult to injury, that offseason I had to have surgery on a knee I injured at the beginning of the season. I was so headstrong that I refused to sit out and played the entire season with a severely hurt knee. We now had a new coach in place and, based on preference and not performance, I was demoted from my starting role. What a devastating blow! This did not fit in with my aspirations to play professional football. I remembered being borderline depressed but, after a few days, I decided to take my mother's advice again and "just do well." I've learned any level of success and leadership that I reached was a result of perseverance and understanding that life is never perfect. You will always have both: success and failure, wins and losses, ups and down. They ultimately mold us into what we were designed to be. It's true that I suffered some losses, but I definitely wouldn't end up a loser.

The Comeback Kid

I had successful knee surgery that offseason and worked like a madman to strengthen my repaired knee. I was able to work myself back into good shape over a few months' period. I started spring practices as a second-string offensive lineman. The first-string guy had been doing really well until one day when he made a series of mistakes that frustrated the coaches. This opened the door for me to get in the game during our annual scrimmage. I knew that was my opportunity to "do well" and I did just that. Once they put me in that day, I never came back out. I went on to start every game I played in the rest of my college career. On the personal side, my step-brother's death brought our family closer together and we began to heal with time. I found a new church near campus and begin to serve in Bible studies and young adult ministry. The key was that the setbacks I experienced never destroyed my desire to move forward. I believe certain things can't be measured and desire is one of them. It means you have an internal resolve to move forward and overcome obstacles at all cost, and that's exactly what I had.

Entering my senior year, I was projected by many scouts to be drafted after the season. Things started off well and everything seemed to be falling into place until the fifth game of the season when I tore the ligaments off my ankle. Just imagine how I felt when I found out that I needed surgery and would have to miss the rest of the season. There I was again, rolling on the ground in severe pain. I would get the chance to go to some camps over the next few years and even play in the Arena Football League. But my dream of making millions as a professional football player was now over. The best thing that came out of this time was meeting my wife of now 12 years at the end of college. She is as stable as they come. She is a great wife and mother to our four children and I couldn't ask for anything better. I thank God for her every day. God knew what was best for me and allowed me to go down the path of marriage and family instead of the fast life of a professional athlete.

Dream Adjust

So what would I do with myself now? Well, I knew one of my strongest gifts was helping and connecting with people. I had received a degree in nutrition and minored in psychology. I knew what I wanted to do… become a big time V.P. at a pharmaceutical company and own my own business. That was definitely easier said than done. I didn't have any contacts in my field of interest and had no experience. No WORRIES! The Great Manufacturer to the rescue. Fully aware of my natural limitations, I knew I had everything inside me I needed to be successful.

Everyone has to start somewhere. I started off selling Yellow Page advertising to businesses. Over the next several months, I rose to be the top salesperson in the office. From there, I took a position in media online advertising, selling to A-list fortune 500 companies. God blessed me greatly there and I achieved 849% of our objective during one of our business cycles. I call that supernatural results. I had enough sales experience at that point to land my first medical sales job. The Great Manufacturer was with me there, too. In under a year, I was #1 in the country in my primary product.

Things were going great until a corporate downsizing forced me to change roles. I moved into a specialty sales role with a smaller company and a larger territory. I worked in multiple medical specialties and had great success across four states. Unfortunately, this company got into some legal trouble and, despite my uncertainty, God once again placed me in a position in the same industry. Even though I had one of the smaller territories and missed three months of work, I was again a national top performer. I realized that God doesn't need a big territory to do big things! One thing about good companies is that they often get sold and that was the case with this company. I was now ready to pursue a different field altogether.

Several days later, I got a phone call and it was from a former co-worker who was starting his own company and wanted me to be the head of his sales division. Wow! I received my greatest breakthrough when I was on the verge of quitting. I accepted and God used me to grow this company exponentially. I became the V.P. of Business Development and Sales, just like I had envisioned. During this time, my wife and I also successfully started a couple of companies and they are doing extremely well. Only God can give you the golden touch.

I enjoy helping youth and teaching them discipline and character through athletics. For the last three years, I've been a volunteer coach in my community and have led several sports teams. In addition to that, I serve in the small group ministry at my church and we hold Bible studies in our home. I take pride in giving back to those who blessed me as a child and look forward to being on a scholarship board for kids to attend college this year. I thank God for His love and goodness in my life and I believe He has even greater things for us all as we attempt to follow him. He makes no mistakes and there are no wasted life experiences. What God has done for one, He will do for another. We are perfectly formed and shaped for His intention in our lives. After all, He is the Great Manufacturer! ■

 CHARLES BEAUFORD *is a father, minister, and entrepreneur. He has four children with his college sweetheart and wife of 12 years and currently serves at his local church. He has worked in the medical field specializing in meeting the needs of clinics and hospitals for the last nine years. Charles is also the CEO of a medical consulting firm designed to help physicians more effectively meet the needs of their patients through innovation strategies that promote a better quality of service and provide more treatment options. Charles is a graduate of the University of Houston and has a degree in nutrition with a minor in psychology.*

He has a passion for helping others to achieve accelerated performance and career excellence with a focus on improving workplace environments. He believes in creating cohesive synergy amongst team members to achieve exceptional results. His calling is to encourage and teach people how to overcome life's obstacles through the love and grace of God. He also has a passion for helping others identify their gifts and talents in order to achieve uncommon results. Charles supports several non-profit organizations such as food pantries, community benevolence initiatives, college scholarship funds, and various Christian ministry endeavors.

His hobbies include working out, cooking, traveling and reading.

Connect with Charles at:
cjbeauford@sbcglobal.net

2

A Camouflaged Soul

Mandy Bourland

Crashing waves on the shoreline of Captiva Island caused an ever-changing beach riddled with the usual ocean contents, seaweed and seashells. As my husband and I walked hand in hand along the water's edge enjoying the beautiful sights and sounds of God's creation, I was on a mission to gather a collection of perfect shells. As the water receded after each wave, I ran toward it in an effort to grab a shell and retreat before the next wave came along. We laughed at the similarity of my behavior to the seabirds running to avoid the deep water while snatching a quick bite from the wet sand. Picking up the shells one by one, I tossed them back into the ocean as I noticed their imperfections. That's when Sandy caught my eye.

He was about the length of my hand, well camouflaged by sand that covered him from head to tail. He wriggled violently, signaling to any passerby that he was fighting for his life. Slightly afraid, but eager to save him, I flung him back into the ocean for a second chance at life. The excitement was overwhelming! "I SAVED A SEAHORSE!" I shouted at least 50 times over the next few hours. I, Mandy Bourland, had made a difference for one of God's creatures! Without me, he would have died right there on that beach. I was meant to walk that section of the beach at that very moment, just for him. I considered "Lucky" for obvious reasons, but decided that "Sandy" would be the perfect name for him. This was an unforgettable moment that would begin my search and emotional connection with any trinket or image of a seahorse. Sandy and I are kindred spirits of sorts.

I, too, have been found many times on the beach of life, covered in sand as the waves of childhood left me in need of rescue. My mother did her very best, I believe, to provide for my brother and me. Looking back, she was empty and had little to give emotionally. She struggled all of her life with depression and low self-esteem. In a constant search for someone to love her unconditionally, she survived six failed marriages. Together, we suffered unique consequences from each one: humiliation, drug use, alcoholism, abandonment, incarceration, and abuse of all kinds.

My mother wanted things to be different for me than they were for her growing up. She had to work incredibly hard in school to even pass. Her father was a police officer and held her to high standards. As a result of her own raising, perfection was the expectation for me at home and at school. It didn't matter how hard I worked, I would always be reprimanded for not doing better.

Chores started early in our house. When my fifth birthday rolled around, hatred began to run deep toward a pink wooden stool that was tied beautifully with a brightly colored ribbon on the gift table that day. Dusting mitts or microfiber cloths were among other "gifts" that I received in my early years. My mother loved to give me cleaning supplies and tools. You know, the things that every kid wishes would be under the Christmas tree. The stool gave me the boost I needed in order to reach the sink to wash dinner dishes. Heaven forbid a dish was taken from the cabinet with a bit of food still on it. If it happened, I washed and dried ALL of the dishes in the kitchen by hand, not just the dirty ones. The same was true of my dresser drawers when they became disorganized. They were dumped in the floor so that I could put it all back the way it was supposed to be. Sounds like a reasonable plan, but my childhood was filled with huge repercussions for what seemed like small mistakes. I tried desperately to gain my mother's approval for years. I longed to hear her say, "You did a good job. I'm proud of you." Those words were very rare and, oh, how self-critical I became. Through my parents' actions, words, and lack of recognition of my effort and accomplishments, I heard the same message over and over until I began to believe it. *I would never be good enough. I must be perfect. Mistakes are unacceptable.* When ridicule and consequences are the result of your most sincere attempts at pleasing your parents, your initiative disappears. Your willingness to break the mold and take risks becomes nonexistent. Creativity is stifled, as the fear of failure becomes the overarching theme in life. This perfectionistic thinking became a part of my identity.

My biological father ran out on us when I was two weeks old, which was probably a blessing in disguise. A few years later, he was incarcerated for armed robbery and attempted murder. Alcoholic husband number four became a part of our world, but that didn't last long. Number five was the worst of all. Since my dad was out of the picture, my step-dad ended up being "daddy" when I was about three. Mom soon began the process for him to officially adopt me through the court system. She thought she was doing a good thing for me. The name Hamner was removed from my birth certificate and replaced with Hughen. This name would become synonymous with humiliation, pain and shame.

Over the next few years, they discovered that I had some bladder problems that caused bed wetting, increased frequency and urgency. My bladder was tiny and wouldn't stretch at all. If I hesitated, I wet my pants. The doctor said that I would grow out of it one day. My dad was not as understanding as my mom. In his eyes, I was lazy and needed to be punished for my choices. I recall a picture, which has since been destroyed, of me lying on my bed without pants in tears after being spanked for wetting my pants. I remember being sent out to play with my wet underwear tied around my neck. Just for the record, it didn't stop my accidents. His plan to humiliate me into keeping dry pants didn't work. I have wondered why my mom didn't step in to protect me from such deliberately cruel treatment, but perhaps she was afraid of him, too.

Fear of physical pain took hold of me because of unusual punishments. I recall spankings on my feet when caught outside barefoot, unexpected swats with a two-by-four when asked to pick up a nail he had dropped on the ground, and the sound of my brother's crying while being spanked in the next room with the buckle end of the belt. Needless to say, we were afraid to upset him and walked on eggshells each and every day. It was a scary way to grow up, but outsiders never knew of the trauma we experienced. Just like Sandy, we blended in. We liked it that way; just to be normal at school felt good. It was our safe haven.

At the age of 10, my innocence was replaced by shame. I should have been able to trust him. After all, he was my daddy. I should have been safe with my daddy, right? He and my mother were in the process of a divorce. At his apartment for the weekend, my world came crashing down around me late one night. I knew it wasn't my fault, but still what he had done changed me forever. I sneaked into the kitchen and called my mom to tell her what had happened. Within minutes the police were everywhere. My dad later went to prison for what he had done to me and to other little girls, including his own sister. As a result of the unhealthy relationships I had with father figures, especially this one, I never knew what a father's love was supposed to be like. This caused difficulty even into adulthood as I struggled to understand the love that my Heavenly Father has for me.

During my years in junior high, my biological father and I began to write back and forth. The letters were filled with promises to come and see me and be a part of my life when he got out of prison. It didn't happen. He promised to send money for school clothes. That didn't happen, either. I began to wonder what was wrong with me. Why does he not want to be a part of my life?

The little girl in me survived a troubled childhood, but was blessed with a heart for others. I have a God-given drive to make a different life for myself. Determination was at the forefront of my mind, to walk a path that my mother did not. I refused to be a failure, to wear a cloak of shame, to be afraid, to believe that I was unworthy. It was clearly communicated to me on several occasions that it was bad news when mom discovered that I was on my way into her life. It was a bad time, in a bad situation, in a bad relationship. But I refused to BE a mistake. God doesn't make mistakes. I chose to believe that I was a beautiful creation of God, made in His image and bound for great things. Clinging to this faith, hope, and love when I had nothing else is what saved my life. It kept my joy alive, my heart open to love, and laid the groundwork for using my wounds to serve others.

I am sharing my story for one purpose—to give hope to those who may have had similar experiences. This is for that hurting soul who feels as if there is no hope. It's for the one thinking that the pain is too great and that the wounds are too deep. I've got news for you! God's got you, so let Him hold you and surround you with angels. He did it for me and he'll do it for you, too! God placed people in my life who picked me up from the sandy beach and tossed me back into the ocean of life: teachers, friends, a counselor, coworkers, a husband and his family. They each gave me a second chance at the life that I deserve. With my story, I should have died on that beach and been one of many different statistics. But I overcame the odds. I broke the cycle.

I am the first in my family to graduate from college and earn a master's degree. I am incredibly blessed with a loyal, devoted, and loving husband who accepts my wounded soul. Through a marriage blessed by God, I have blossomed in so many ways. I have confidence and peace that did not previously exist. Abandonment is no longer heavy on my heart. I know unconditional love and acceptance and strive to show my son the value in mistakes. I finally understand what a parent's love feels like. God reminds me of His love each and every time I look at my precious son. That unconditional love and acceptance that He has for me, even in my brokenness, is far more immeasurable than I could possibly imagine. My career in the field of education has provided me with a multitude of opportunities to pick up little seahorses (and even some big ones) on the beach and throw them back into the ocean. I am placing a challenge before you today: look for the sand-covered seahorses around you. They may be camouflaged, but they are there. You can be a difference maker. ■

MANDY BOURLAND *is a wife and mother committed to raising her son in a home with a strong marriage and family built on God's love. Spending time with family playing games is her favorite use of spare time. She attended University of North Texas where she earned a Bachelor of Interdisciplinary Studies and Master's in Educational Administration. Since 2000, she has served in the field of elementary education as teacher, instructional specialist, and administrator. Mandy is devoted to servant leadership, continuous improvement, and building relationships to maximize success in schools. By inspiring people to approach others with grace, she promotes a positive learning and working environment. Mandy has a dedicated heart for children and finds healing and joy in working with them in public school and at church. She works extensively with teachers to share an open-minded perspective for students who experience adverse childhood experiences and how their learning is affected. Mandy is dedicated to using each interaction as an opportunity to share a message of hope and love.*

Mandy Bourland
mandy1023@att.net
www.mandybourland.com
972-658-0139

3

I WONDER...Or At Least I Used To
Marcus Bourland

One day in my office I needed a book on the top shelf of the built-in bookcase. The book was just out of my reach. This is a common situation realized by many. I had faced this routine dilemma on many occasions. But this day proved to be a very uncommon and crucial experience, changing the way I viewed the world and how I present this world to others.

A little background information is important to sincerely appreciate the book predicament. It is my belief that we are the sum total of our experiences. It is important to understand some of my experiences to explain why I would see a life-changing experience because a book is located on the top shelf.

My parents were astounding. I had a mother who viewed the world differently than most. Every sunset was "the most amazing thing" that she had ever seen. Sitting in the swing in the backyard to watch nature was a daily routine, and she viewed each day the way many view the Super Bowl that happens only once a year. I spent a lot of time sitting in the swing with her while learning to marvel at God's creation. She brought this excitement about the world to her classroom as an elementary school teacher. Her excitement for life inspired each student to learn in the classroom in the same way I learned during those long talks in the swing. My mother is truly wonderful and full of wonder. Please, hold onto that thought or, as I tell students, "bookmark your brain."

As my dad would hear my mom speak of a sunset, he would often say, "It is just a sunset." He does not have the same perspective on nature; however, the way he views people is remarkable. My dad was a tremendous preacher and pastor. I list these separately only for emphasis. As a preacher, he studied God's Word and shared the Word with the congregation. As a pastor, he ministered to people often in the hour of their greatest need. This ministry included general support, prayer and counseling, frequently in times of illness or death. I wanted to go with my dad everywhere he went and would beg that he wait to go to the hospitals until I was home from school. I watched him and joined in as he ministered to people and witnessed firsthand him marveling at God's creation of human beings. His passion for caring for and loving people set him apart and touched the lives of so many. My dad was truly wonderful and full of wonder. This is another bookmark for your brain. Soon we will get back to the book on the top shelf.

Let's give credit where credit is due. My mother taught me to view all of nature and the workings of this world as a spectacular creation to be enjoyed and marveled every day. She also showed me how imperative it is that we share this knowledge with all those who will listen. If the response is "it is only a sunset," I will then try even harder to bring alive the wonder in that person. My dad taught me to love and care for people and to realize that each person is an impressive creation, no matter how his or her experiences are displayed.

Each of my parents gave me an example of living beyond the norm in their love of the creation and how they expressed that to the world around them. This brought about captive audiences in both schools and in the churches. They were different and people knew it. I blame, or probably more positively put, attribute, my non-conformist ways to my parents. They were different, so I wanted to be different. My parents' examples inspired me to intentionally live out a life full of wonder.

I am a high school administrator. The book and the shelf were in my office, the principal's office. Administrators start out as teachers, and the great ones remain teachers at heart. As a teacher, I was labeled as "Crazy Bourland." I walked on tables, rode my scooter in the classroom and hallways, stood in chairs and used Nerf™ guns to arouse drowsy students. It was so important to me to share the excitement for how the world works and to share my love for each student as they walked through the door. I found that by being different, or "crazy," as the students labeled it, created an intrigued audience. Learning does not occur without audience. I believe that educators have a full-time job striving to bring audiences to wonder. Once they are full of wonder the education becomes easy. Ultimately, some of the students may have watched closely just to see if I would fall out of the chair or off of the table. For the record, it only happened once and it was epic.

Now I am an administrator and I am still proud that my scooter is displayed on a shelf. My approach to students in the classroom and my approach to adults are to be different enough to bring others to the state of wonder. I found that all audiences want to be intrigued.

The book was on the top shelf and I could not reach it. What happened next? I grabbed a chair and moved it over to assist me with the vertical challenge. I know this is common, but in that moment, it was a tragic realization. Why did it seem natural to stop being a non-conformist and give up a little of my wonder? Why did I reach for the chair? Why did I not just JUMP to get the book? There is no physical reason preventing me from leaping for the book just out of reach. I realized I had made a choice for the norm and given up on a little of the craziness. Is this what happens as we get older? Does the wonder stop before the physical challenges of bad backs and achy knees?

After that day, I became even more determined to intentionally maintain my own wonder and encourage wonder in the lives of others. Wonder is a very powerful emotion. For example, watch how easy it is to educate young children. They are full of wonder and this makes them hungry for knowledge. Wouldn't you like your students, clients, or audiences to be more full of wonder? What would this do to increase their desire to learn and the level of your impact?

Displaying one's wonder is somewhat contagious, but how do we intentionally stimulate wonder in others? Can you use this incredible tool to reach others with your message? When educating students and adults, ultimately we try to present information that brings wonder enough to leave any audience wanting to know more. This is true in all industries, business, sales, ministry, and education. When audiences of any kind are brought to wonder, the door is open for the message.

Public speaking, educating and training are passions for me to have the opportunity to share with students and adults about education, life and relationships. I love to speak to groups and see them smile and lean forward to hear a message, letting me know that a little wonder has been created. It is the wonder that I intentionally stir in them.

Wonder is developed in others by first displaying your own wonder to the world. I have done this by taking advantage of doing the things that never ceased to be fun but somehow got labeled, "I am too old for that stuff." I have gotten immeasurable enjoyment out of a Toys-R-Us gift card, well used, in the purchase of my yellow and black scooter. The fact that I have a Toys-R-Us gift card, as an adult, is proof that people around me know that I am wonder-full.

My scooter is proudly displayed in my office and is ridden as often as possible. Audiences of students or adults are immediately interested in what this guy riding the scooter is going to say. When riding in the halls at school the same question always comes up, "Why do you have a scooter?" Isn't the answer somewhat universal, "because it is fun"? If the answer is universal, then why do people ask? It is because others are really asking why you have a scooter in your late thirties. The universal answer remains.

When the scooter comes into question, I love to ask, "Would you like to ride it?" The response is often accompanied by a facial expression of meekness and joy when they say, "Can I?" as if they need my permission to wonder because somehow they have outgrown it.

A toddler lives in a constant state of wonder. Everything is new and exciting. As we get older, some of the wonder is jaded out of us and for others it is lost because of the fast-paced lives we lead. When we are educated and become accustomed to the wonders around us, we often take them for granted. For example, the huge cumulus clouds on a bright sunny day inspire in children to see puppies or dragons in the shapes that are formed. Often, adults find it no less fascinating; they just do not take the time to look up. An adult reminded and given time to stop and wonder can become a captive audience.

The desire to wonder is natural for all. The entertainment industry is based on engaging a world of wonder seekers. Audiences use money to spend time in a world of wonder through movies, live shows and concerts. We want our lives to be more full of wonder. Vacations are spent seeking out the wonder in the world. Think about how you feel when you see a mountain view with the majestic trees and rocks all around, or standing on the beach as the ocean waves crash against the shore. You marvel and wonder at these sights.

Why do we need to wonder? A scientist may view this as our DNA driven by a need to evolve. I believe that we were made by our Creator to wonder. God made each one of us with a spirit that leads to Him. Here is the proof. We are amazed and brought to wonder by the things that demonstrate significance beyond ourselves. When we see the mountains, outer space, or the ocean, we realize that we are infinitely insignificant to a much greater plan. Strangely, this brings us peace rather than anxiety. This is not intuitive, but rather God-designed.

As a leader in any field, we need to show the world our own wonder and be intentional in leading others to wonder. When presenting information to a group the message will be heard, appreciated and remembered when wonder is created. It is not the expectation the readers will all purchase scooters and ride them around. Not every situation calls for a scooter. I learned this when taking my scooter to a job interview. Let's just say it was the"elephant in the room."

This discussion of wonder has been based on the"Why?"It is my intention to build the case for the need and usefulness of inspiring wonder in others. My hope is to spend the rest of my career accomplishing this with audiences of all ages. I will be outlining more of the "Why?" and the "How?" in an upcoming book. This book will further explain why inspiring wonder helps parents, educators, businessmen, salesmen, or ministers reach people and develop relationships.

My greatest passion is to demonstrate these principles while speaking, in ministry or secular environments, using a variety of subject matters including presenting motivational content, building relationships in business and personal lives, and equipping students to make it in a challenging world, both with parent and student audiences. God has given me the ability to connect with audiences of all ages. I truly believe this is based on the childlike wonder that I never lost. Others can learn to recapture wonder and share it.

Dare to be a difference maker by intentionally sustaining wonder in your life and inspiring others to do the same. ■

MARCUS BOURLAND *earned a Bachelor of Business Administration degree and Master's degree in Educational Leadership from University of North Texas. He has been a business owner and worked in business sales. For the past 10 years he has served in public education as a teacher and administrator. He is married to his high school sweetheart that is a love that has grown over 23 years. He and his wife see the wonder of God's creation through the eyes of a precious son. Marcus loves to share insights in life from experiences as a preacher's kid, businessman and owner, teacher, and school administrator. He is a passionate speaker that connects with audiences of educators, students, parents, businesses and churches, using humor and unique style. He has a childlike wonder and brings the wonder out in others.*

Marcus Bourland
marcusbourland@rocketmail.com
www.marcusbourland.com
972-658-3168

4

A Life Blessed
Mike Bowman

I want to begin by saying how blessed my life has been. Without the Lord's help, there is no way I could've had the success that I've had. I also have been blessed with a wonderful and supportive wife of 51 years, three children, seven grandchildren, and two great-grandchildren.

I was born in Vincennes, Indiana, on September 28, 1942. My dad's cousin joined the Navy and asked my dad to keep his car for him until he got back. When I was born, my dad didn't have enough money to pay the hospital bill, so he sold his cousin's car to pay the bill to get my mom and me out of the hospital.

My folks lived in Washington, Indiana, where my dad worked on the B&O Railroad. He was a hardworking man and working on the railroad was a very tough job. Whether it was hot, cold, rain, or snow, he was out in the weather. He was gone every two to three days, and back home one, then gone again. My mother was a stay-at-home mom. She was an angel and supported me in all my challenges. I was an only child surrounded by great parents, grandparents, aunts and uncles. Being the oldest grandchild among both grandparents, I enjoyed being spoiled by everyone. Both my parents were from Lawrenceville, Illinois.

Washington, Indiana, was a small-time town that was sports-crazy, especially when it came to the game of basketball. Growing up I played in many different sports and worked with local farmers in mending fences, planting, and just regular farm work. I received several scholar-ships in football after graduating from high school, but decided to attend the small two-year college, Vincennes University, in Vincennes, Indiana. Vincennes University was 18 miles from Washington, Indiana, and 10 miles from Lawrenceville, Illinois.

The day I graduated from high school, I moved to Lawrenceville to work with my uncle Roy Boles in construction. Roy was a World War II vet and a very hard worker. Everyone loved him because he always delivered better than expected services when people hired him. My time with my Uncle Roy was very valuable. There were three things that he taught me about work. (1) He always laughed when he would say, "Always leave the wood pile stacked higher than when you found it." (2) "Can't never did anything," and (3) "Never quit on accomplishing your dreams."

One of the special events while work-ing with my uncle was when we got the opportunity to paint a very old church in Vincennes, Indiana, called Saint Francis Xavier Cathedral, also known as the Old Cathedral. This church was founded in the mid 1700s and one day while I was eating my lunch outside, I saw a grave marker. The grave marker name was Major Joseph Bowman. I was shocked to see the name Bowman on this stone. That evening, when I was talking to my grandfather Bow-man, I said, "Did you know there was a grave marker with the name of Major Joseph Bowman at the Old Cathedral church in Vin-cennes?" His reply was that during the Revolutionary War, several Bowmans fought with George Rogers Clark, and they had taken over Fort

Vincennes from the British and that Major Joseph Bowman was the only fatality (1779). He said to his knowledge, from parents and grandparents, that these Bowmans who fought with George Rogers Clark during the Revolutionary War were distant relatives of ours.

Uncle Roy was raised in North Carolina in a very poor home. At the end of World War II, he was stationed at Georgefield Military Base, outside of Lawrenceville, where he met my dad's sister, Marge Bowman. Back in North Carolina, Uncle Roy had several brothers and sisters. One of his younger brothers was Billy Joe Boles, who the family helped finish college. Billy Joe joined the Air Force and was sent to Vietnam and, through the years, rose to the rank of Four-Star General over all personnel in the Air Force. He is now retired and enjoying the good life.

My mom had three brothers who lived in Texas. In the summer of 1963, my mom's brother Nathaniel Neal and his family came back to Lawrenceville for a visit. He encouraged me to move to Texas, claiming there were lots of job opportunities for me. My mom, dad, and I visited Fort Worth, Texas, when I was 13 years old, and something inside me said this was where I would settle down. During that summer, I was dating my girlfriend, Jan David. We had dated for approximately two years and decided to get married in August. After the wedding and with $300 in my pocket, we decided to go to Hot Springs, Arkansas, for our honeymoon. After a few days there, I talked my newly-wedded wife Jan into going to Fort Worth, Texas, for a visit with my aunts and uncles. When we arrived in Fort Worth, my Uncle Nat said he could get me a job at Bell Helicopter in engineering. My education at Vincennes University was in pre-engineering, and my goal was to be an aeronautical engineer. To my surprise, my uncle got me an appointment with Art Kampshafer, who was the supervisor over the weights group in engineering. Before my interview, my uncle gave me some advice. He said that if the supervisor's last question was, "Do you play golf?" I should respond with "yes." I'd actually never even set foot on a golf course before. But my uncle said if I wanted the job, I'd have to say, "Yes, I play golf."

Waiting downstairs to meet Mr. Kampshafer, I was very nervous. It was hard for me to believe that I had an appointment with a supervisor in the engineering department at Bell Helicopter. When I sat down in front of Mr. Kampshafer, the first words out of his mouth were, "We are not really hiring anyone in the engineering department without an engineering degree." I explained to him that I had two years pre-engineering from Vincennes University in Vincennes, Indiana. He then asked if I would be willing to finish my education. I answered in the affirmative. I then said, "What would the job entail?" He said that a lot of mathematics was involved. I asked him if he would give me a math test involving mathematical problems that would be involved in the job. If I passed, consider me. If I don't pass, I'll understand.

After I finished the math test and he was looking over my paperwork, he looked at me and asked, "Do you play golf?" I hesitated for a moment, and then I said, "Yes, I do." Mr. Kampshafer responded, "You're hired, and we have a golf tournament next week. You'll start to work on Monday." I could not believe what he had just said to me. I was overwhelmed. That evening, everyone was excited about my new job, except for my wife, Jan. She was not expecting for us to live in the Fort Worth area, far away from her family in Illinois. My problem was I didn't have any golf clubs, but I knew that Jan's brother, Jim David, played golf. So I called Jim, who was in Lawrenceville, and asked him if I could borrow his golf clubs. He agreed and sent them by Greyhound Bus, and I picked them up on Saturday in Fort Worth. Without ever hitting a golf ball, I was to play my first game of golf after not being honest with my supervisor. Although no one on the team knew how nervous I was, my sports background enabled me to keep up. They never knew the real story.

I was at Bell Helicopter from 1963 to 1969. In 1963, Jan was having a hard time adjusting to Texas. She made several trips back to her hometown of Lawrenceville while her grandfather was ill with cancer. After a few months in Texas, Jan decided she wanted to move back to Lawrenceville. I told her I already made a commitment to Bell Helicopter and this was where I needed to be. There was a phone booth outside of our apartment where she called home on a regular basis. This time she was calling to tell her parents she was coming back home. To her surprise, it was her dad who answered the phone. Normally, he was at work during this time of day. "Dad," she said, "I'm coming home. Texas doesn't agree with me very well."There was a long pause. Then Bill David replied, "Honey, you can come home but no one will be there to meet you. You are married to Mike and have made that commitment to him and you are not welcome here at home." Jan dropped the receiver in the phone booth, came back to our apartment, gave me that look of disappointment and said, "I'm not welcome back in Lawrenceville so I guess I'll be making my permanent home here in Texas with you."

In November of 1963, while at work (my wife Jan was in Lawrenceville), news spread rapidly through the engineering department that President John F. Kennedy had just been shot. That evening, I went by my aunt and uncle's home to watch the news. No one could believe that such a thing could happen to our president. Then a few days later, as I was watching TV, Jack Ruby shot Lee Harvey Oswald, the person who was accused of shooting the president. It was a terrible time, and it happened just a few miles from where I was working.

After six years at Bell Helicopter, three children, and Jan beginning to like Texas, everything was going well. We had a new home, a new car, and money in the bank. Then late one afternoon at work, Art called me into his office and asked me to take a seat. "Mike, engineering is reducing the amount of employees, and I have no choice but to lay you off. I'm giving you early notice so you can look for a job."

I soon got an offer to move to Atlanta, Georgia, with Lockheed as a job shopper on the C5A cargo plane. My wife was unhappy about that. During my time at Bell Helicopter, I received my pilot's license, commercial license, multi-engine rating, and I could possibly go to work for Braniff Airlines where some of my pilot friends had already gotten jobs. Moving to Georgia didn't seem to be an option, and flying for Braniff I would have been away from home a lot and I had already experienced that with my dad working on the railroad. My next thought was that I wanted to look into some kind of sales position.

After several job interviews, all my interviewers said that engineers don't make good sales representatives. A close friend told me that he had a friend who was a real estate broker named Brian Anderson and that I should talk to him about getting my real estate license. When I interviewed with Brian, he said that if I passed my real estate exam that he would be my sponsoring broker. After passing the exam, I was now a REALTOR. It was a lot different than working at Bell Helicopter as an engineer. Now, I was actually in business for myself, and I had to work up a plan to succeed. I asked Brian, "What do I do now?" His reply was, "Here is your desk, here is the phone, start making calls." In amazement, I asked him again, "I don't understand, what do I do?" His reply was, "Hand out as many cards as you can each day, try to find those prospects who are ready to buy a home or sell a home." That sounded like a good plan, so I ordered 5,000 business cards. My goal was to hand out 167 cards a day, knocking on doors and handing out a card to everyone I met. When I knocked on the door and no one was home, I would leave the card on the door and write on the back "Please call me." Within a few days, I was having several prospects call me about their real estate needs.

That first year, I worked with a lot of builders including a builder named Bob McGar. Toward the end of my first year in real estate, Bob asked me to join him and help him build a real estate office to sell his homes. In approximately one year I had recruited 23 agents and we were selling a lot of Bob McGar homes. After passing my broker's test in 1971, I informed Bob McGar that I was going to open up my own real estate company. I went to see my banker to borrow $6,000, and they turned me down.

While I was working at Bell Helicopter, I met Polly Dobkins. She introduced me to her husband, Searcy, who was in real estate and banking. Searcy had kept in contact with me when I first went into real estate. The day that I got turned down by my banker for the $6,000 loan, Searcy stopped by Bob McGar's office. He was always checking with me to see how I was doing and from time to time he would give me one of his properties to list for sale. I told him about receiving my broker's license and wanting to open up my own real estate office. I told him about my banker turning me down for a $6,000 loan. He looked at me for a minute and then said, "Go see Chuck Gage at First State Bank, and see if he will make you a loan." I called and set an appointment for the next day. When Mr. Gage introduced himself, he asked what I needed. I told him that I wanted to open my own real estate company and I needed $6,000 to get started. He reached for some papers on his desk. When he turned the papers around, they were loan documents that read "$6,000 loan to Mike Bowman."

Immediately, Searcy Dobkins' name flashed into my head. Later I found out that Searcy was a director at this bank, and he had guaranteed this loan. All I needed to do was sign the papers, and my dream of owning my own real estate company would come true. I immediately got on the phone and called Searcy to thank him for the help. I told him I wouldn't let him down. His reply was that he had watched me for two years with a great desire and passion in growing my business. His response was that "I'm a gambling man. This is not a gamble, this is a sure thing."

I opened my first office at 333 Bedford-Euless Road in Hurst, Texas. The number three has always been my lucky number, and I had no idea of the address when I signed the lease for 500 square feet. I immediately got to work listing and selling real estate, recruiting new agents, training them, paying all the bills, cleaning the office, and whatever else needed to get done. As the office grew, we became more and more competitive with other brokers and agents.

In 1975, with approximately 35 agents, I was approached by Joe Foster who had just purchased the CENTURY 21 region and franchise rights for Texas, Oklahoma, Arkansas, and Louisiana. I was one of the first brokers to sign a CENTURY 21 Franchise Agreement in the four-state region. CENTURY 21 had started in California in the early '70s and was rapidly expanding across the country. It turned out to be a very good business decision. After expanding and outgrowing my office space of 1,500 square feet, I moved to Norwood in Bedford, Texas, and occupied two locations. I was at one location for three years and had approximately 3,500 square feet of office space, and after outgrowing this location, I moved across the street to another location with 6,000 square feet of office space for four years. In 1983, I partnered with three attorneys and moved into a 72,000 square foot building on Westpark Way in Euless. CENTURY 21 Mike Bowman, Inc., occupied 12,000 square feet of that building with more than 85 agents. My goal was to have a single office with over 100 agents. At that time, most brokers had several small offices with 10 to 12 agents in each office. To me that was not the way to grow my business.

During the '80s and '90s, we grew to well over 100 agents. In our new location, we started to analyze each department in our company and worked on ways to improve and implement technology to help our agents be more productive. We were one of the first to design and implement a leads management and seller feedback model for the real estate industry.

In 1993, we developed an in-house software program, iBroker, which would run the front office and back office and would assist the agents in managing their business. We included a customer service system with leads management, appointment setting, and seller feedback systems— one of the first in the country. The leads management system became a major part of our growth by staying in touch with potential buyers and sellers continually until they were ready to move to the next level. The software included an appointment-setting module that enabled the front desk to set appointments for agents on our listings and other brokers' listings through our appointment-setting coordinators. The seller feedback module was developed to keep sellers informed on the likes and dislikes that buyers had about their property. A staff member would call each agent that showed one of our properties to get feedback from their buyer about our listing. This saved the agents many hours in trying to follow up with agents that showed their listings to get that information back to their seller. By streamlining the feedback process, this helped notify the seller on anything they needed to improve with their property to help it sell faster by upgrading the condition or adjusting the pricing.

Since I started my real estate office in 1971, the key ingredients to having a successful real estate office are (1) continually recruit new and experienced agents, (2) develop a well-educated training department that can motivate and teach the agents how to become professional salespeople, and (3) develop a well-trained staff that can assist and support the agents. That has always been the key to our success. We again moved our office in 2006 to our new building in Grapevine, Texas, with over 220 agents and staff. We have become one of the top real estate companies in the nation. CENTURY 21 Mike Bowman, Inc., has been the number one CENTURY 21 office 18 times in the CENTURY 21 system. I have just celebrated my 45th year as a REALTOR and broker; 43 years owning my own brokerage and 39 years as a top company in the CENTURY 21 Worldwide system. We have helped tens of thousands of buyers and sellers move in and out of the Dallas-Fort Worth area. I have helped thousands of agents achieve a successful career in this awesome profession. Each REALTOR who comes to work for CENTURY 21 Mike Bowman, Inc., is our partner and teammate. It is my obligation as a broker, and the management team's, to do everything we possibly can to help each individual achieve the level of success that they aspire to. It is all about people helping people achieve financial success and living a better life. As I said in the beginning, I have been very blessed.

Joseph Bowman (c. 1752 – c. 14 August 1779) was a Virginia militia officer during the American Revolutionary War. He was second-in-command during George Rogers Clark's famous campaign to capture the Illinois country, in which Clark and his men seized the British-controlled towns of Kaskaskia, Vincennes, and others. Bowman was injured in an accidental gunpowder explosion after the campaign, and subsequently died of his wounds. He was the only American officer killed during the Illinois campaign. Bowman kept a daily journal during the trek from Kaskaskia to Vincennes, which is one of the best primary accounts of the event.

MIKE BOWMAN. *I was raised in Washington, Indiana, where I graduated from high school in 1961. I went to the two-year college at Vincennes University in Vincennes, Indiana, where I studied pre-engineering.*

I married my lovely wife Jan in August of 1963 and moved to Dallas/Fort Worth, Texas, with a new bride and $300. I put my application in for a position in the engineering department at Bell Helicopter. I was immediately hired for a position in the weights group. I worked there from 1963 to 1969 when, due to not having a degree in engineering, I was laid off.

My wife and I at that time had a new home, new car, and three new kids. I obtained my real estate salesman's license and sold real estate during 1969 and 1970. In 1971 I opened my own real estate office. I started listing and selling real estate, recruiting, managing all the accounting, and the many other jobs within the office. In 1975, I joined the CENTURY 21® Franchise System. Our company continued to grow through the 1980s and 1990s.

In 1993, we started developing an in-house software program called iBroker to run the back and front office, leads management follow-up system, and a seller feedback system for our company. In 2006, we moved to our new location in Grapevine, Texas, with over 223 agents and staff. We have become one of the top real estate companies in the nation and have been named the #1 office 18 times in the world-wide CENTURY 21® System. I've just celebrated my 46th year as a REALTOR® and Broker and in August of this year, my wife and I will celebrate our 52nd wedding anniversary.

Mike Bowman, President
Mike Bowman, Inc.
mike@c21bowman.com
817-354-7653

5

Make A Difference, Let Your Light Shine
Beverly Woodson Day, Ph.D.

This story is about the light that each of us has and who we share that light with. You will find that friendship is priceless, family is genuine, and children are a blessing from above. The life you live determines the type of light that shines through you and how it affects those around you. This story should encourage you so that your light shines brighter every day.

> *For God, who said, "Let there be light in the darkness," has made this light shine in our hearts so we could know the glory of God that is seen in the face of Jesus Christ. We now have this light shining in our hearts, but we ourselves are like fragile clay jars containing this great treasure. This makes it clear that our great power is from God, not from ourselves.*
>
> *2 Corinthians 4: 6-7*

I sat in the cold, dark room of the ICU surrounded by white walls and beeping machines. I looked at my friend as she lay in a hospital bed, my friend of 14 years. This feisty, full of life, adventurous woman lay there, fighting that evil disease called cancer. She didn't say much and neither did I. We were just listening to the silence and enjoying the moment. I looked at her and she smiled, mouthing, "love you." I said it back softly, "love you." A moment later I told her to rest, reassuring her that I would be there for awhile. She closed her eyes, drifted off to sleep, and I sat back in the chair, letting out a long breath. I looked at her and thought to myself, *my friend is an inspiration of light*. I sat there watching her and thinking of all of the people she touched. How her life and the light she carried shined through her and brightened many lives. The lives of her students, her friends, and her family. I began to think of how her light inspired and touched me. How our time spent together was priceless, and how many of our conversations were in-depth and the stories we shared ended with laughing so hard we cried. How I learned so much from listening to her and realizing her dreams and aspirations and, at the same time, finding mine. In our years together, she entered my world and I entered hers and we became great colleagues and close friends. I sat there giving thanks for her life and her light touching my life.

My mind began to drift and I began to think of who might have touched my life and how the light they carried was shared with me. I thought about my grandparents. Their impact on my life was amazing. I remember growing up with Mawmaw and Pawpaw Jones. I recall how they would treat other people, welcome neighbors into their circle, and share their kind-heartedness with friends and, many times, those in need. They were well known for their giving spirit and noble character. I remember going to their home often and always walking out into their garden, the garden they planted every year. That garden that took time, patience and commitment. Year after year, tilling, planting and harvesting. I learned a lot from them. That whatever you do requires a system and time. It was like the garden. It took time to till, plant and harvest. It took commitment, patience and hard work to, in the end, produce a quality product. They taught me how to work hard, be a giver, have patience and stay committed.

My grandparents on the Mathis side focused on the importance of family. Spending quality time, whether it was at a family reunion or some other occasion; they believed in keeping family together. Anytime I would visit them with my parents, there would always be family around. I would see family I was related to and those that weren't related, but were treated as such. They taught me that time spent with family should be enjoyable and energizing. A time to celebrate, be thankful, and just have a good ol' time. I realize that the life and light my grandparents shared with me developed how I live my life today; always enjoying family, having a patient spirit, staying committed and forever giving.

My friend stirred for a moment, but didn't wake. I sat up to make sure she didn't need anything and, once I realized she was fine, I sat back in the chair and my mind drifted to my parents. To think they came together, shared their light and love, and gave me life. They continue to share so much with me and my siblings. Their wisdom and knowledge of life in general, what to do and what not to do, how to be a parent and trust in God. I laugh every time I think of the funny things they say or do. I think about how for 44 years their marriage continues to stand, tall and strong like a lighthouse, withstanding the storms of life, being a pillar of strength, and serving as a guiding light for others on the outside looking in.

I came back to reality as my friend shifted in the bed. She opened her eyes and reached for my hand. I sat up in the chair and grabbed hers. I held on and she squeezed tightly. Words can never express how just being present in the moment makes a difference. We stayed like that for a moment and she released my hand and drifted back to sleep. I sat back in the chair and began to think of my son.

What a good, kind-hearted kid. I see his light shining daily. He has a goal and a passion for something that far surpasses anything I could ever dream of. His passion is to go to the Olympics. About two years ago, he found his love—International Skeet. He said, "Mom, when I win the gold...," and I believe and know he can do it. He has this passion and he shares that with us daily. I knew he was special from day one.

I vividly recall a time while traveling for my job, I had a layover one weekend that afforded me time to spend with a dear friend of mine. It was a Sunday and she asked me to go to church with her. I, of course, said yes. It was a wonderful service, but the one thing that made it spectacular was something the pastor did. He asked all those expecting to come to the front to receive a blessing for their child. I hesitated for a moment, because I hadn't told my friend yet, but something told me, *get up and get that blessing on this child*. I did, and she almost fell out of her seat. She looked at me and I smiled. I went up to the front with a handful of others, and received a blessing on my son. I believe that moment made a difference in his life and mine. But as I think about where he is today, the drive, the determination, and the vision that he has to be an Olympic Gold Medalist shines bright. I see him training hard, working harder, and getting stronger. Both his dad and I work at keeping him focused, doing what we can to help him train and showing and sharing our enthusiasm. As teenagers, their lives can be so complicated and overbearing with school, relationships, homework and such, but thinking about how strongly he believes in himself, this mere teenager has helped me appreciate the passion he has and that he shares with me. I know that the light I was given from my grandparents and parents has been passed down to him to continue to carry the torch on for generations.

I think of the lives I have shared my life and light with. The countless students I mentored and counseled regarding college, their relationships, and their future. The many leadership conferences that were organized to prepare students for life lessons. The organizations I advised to prepare the members for leadership roles. I thought of the lives my friend touched as she taught master's courses at the university and presented workshops at numerous conferences. All of this not to hide, but to share and shine the light that was given to us.

My thoughts drifted back to ICU as darkness became light as the nurse entered the room. I looked at the clock and figured it was time to go. I got up and as the nurse was preparing my dear friend for the night, I grabbed her hand, kissed her head and thought to myself, *thank you for this moment in time and for sharing your light with me*. I left that room, not with a heavy heart but with a joy-filled heart, realizing that light brings life. Although our life at one point in time will come to an end, the light that we have been blessed with in our hearts should be shared with others. I left there with a different meaning of what light truly means and how life can live on through light.

Fast-forward a few weeks. My dear, close friend lost her fight with cancer. It may have taken her from us but her light continues to shine in everyone and everything she touched. I found myself sitting in Christmas Eve service with my family and listening to a message on Christmas lights. *John 1:9 says, "The one who is the true light, who gives light to everyone, was coming into the world."* I thought about that and thought of all of the lights in my world: my friends, my parents, my grandparents, my sons, my siblings, my husband, and even people I have yet crossed paths with. Each of us has that light in our life that makes a difference, touches us in some way, and changes our life. Share your life and let your light shine to make a difference in someone's life.

> *"You are the light of the world—like a city on a hilltop that cannot be hidden. No one lights a lamp and then puts it under a basket. Instead, a lamp is placed on a stand, where it gives light to everyone in the house. In the same way, let your good deeds shine out for all to see, so that everyone will praise your heavenly Father."*
>
> *Matthew 5:14-16*

BEVERLY WOODSON DAY, PH.D.

Beverly has worked in higher education for over 20 years. She spent the majority of her career at Texas State University where she held various positions. She is a graduate of Texas State University with a Bachelor's in Physics, a Master's in Developmental and Adult Education, and a Doctorate in Adult, Professional, and Community Education.

She is published in the Journal of Higher Education for research on faculty perceptions of adult students. Leadership and mentoring have been her passion for years. For 19 years she advised the African American Leadership Conference at Texas State, equipping thousands of students with leadership skills. Beverly is involved in several state and national associations; serving on committees, presenting at conferences, and holding numerous leadership positions.

She serves as the Higher Ed Curriculum Chair for Texas Association for College Admission Counseling's Admissions and College Counseling Institute (ACCI), which prepares new professionals for a range of experiences as university representatives. Currently, she serves as President of TACAC. Beverly is the Director of Admissions at the University of Texas at San Antonio, where she continues to encourage and develop students and staff. Beverly supports her husband Tracy with his motivational speaking and financial service careers, and their children in their life endeavors.

Beverly Woodson Day, Ph.D.
Beverly@TracyDayMotivation.com

6

Beeing Blessed: A Sunshine Maker

Amanda M. Ferris

Have you ever thought *This is NOT how I wanted my life to be! I've been DUPED—this ISN'T what I signed up for!* or, *Is this ALL there IS?*

Straight from my heart to yours, life can be everything you have wanted and more—it CAN change!

I admit, some of what you're about to read may not be what you expect to find in a book about "difference-makers." But the truth is, my past was instrumental in getting me to where I am today—and the lessons I've learned can help you get to where you want to be, too.

By putting aside the fear and anxiety of sharing my times of shame, hopelessness, and fear, I can illustrate the core principles that altered the trajectory of my life to where I am now—consistently living in the realm of possibility and loving joy.

If you are reading this, I believe that we are kindred spirits and friends that have not yet met. If you haven't yet started on the path of pursuing your dreams by living your passions before today, TODAY is your starting point, and I am here to cheer you on!

A Little Background

I was raised in a suburb just a few minutes south of Minneapolis/St. Paul. My family consisted of my mom and dad, as well as my younger sister and brother. My mom was an award-winning in-home licensed daycare provider, and my dad was a dedicated skilled-trades employee at one of the big auto manufacturers.

I was raised in a suburb just a few minutes south of Minneapolis/St. Paul. My family consisted of my mom and dad, as well as my younger sister and brother.

I always looked up to my parents, admiring their hard work and love of life, and from an early age was compelled to follow their example of kindness and generosity. My parents married at ages 18 and 19, and delivered all of their children within the first three years of their marriage. Though they experienced significant personal and financial hardships early on, they each became successful in their professions after just a few years of struggle. They have always wanted the best for me, and made many sacrifices to support me. Even in the moments before I was born, my teen-aged parents were faced with the choice of whether my mother or I would be the one to survive the labor—and they both agreed that it would be me. It was a doctor-acknowledged act of God that we both lived through the emergency C-section, and without any lasting health issues. I am absolutely grateful that I was brought into this world and brought up by these two incredible people. Like any other kid, I dealt with sibling rivalries, typical peer group issues, requisite growing pains and awkwardness, but both parents reminded me on a regular basis that they loved me, they were proud of me, and that I could be ANYTHING in life that I could dream of. My childhood memories are filled with laughter, fun family activities, and adventures all over the world.

Then, everything changed.

Every so often, we would hear "FAMILY MEETING!" echo throughout our home. This meant *drop what you're doing and get to the living room NOW—or ELSE.* The most common topics included new household responsibilities, announcements about extended family, and upcoming family events.

But one day, the family meeting included a new word in our household. *Divorce.*

Looking back, there had been signs: My mother crying during a tension-filled vacation, my father being out of town during the family Christmas celebration.

As a little girl, I saw my parents in an almost super-hero light. I wanted to grow up to be just like them—innovative and adventurous like my dad, beautiful and fun like my mom. But life didn't turn out the way they had planned, either, and despite their very best efforts to give us the world and hold this facade together for us, reality crept in.

Immediately after my parents announced their divorce, I began to question each value and virtue they had ever promoted. If this whole family thing was a sham, then everything else had to be as well. *Why should I care anymore? No one loves me or wants me, and they lied to me my entire life! I played by the rules—I'm supposed to have a happy life! This isn't fair!* I thought.

The stress of a crumbling family left me feeling alienated and unworthy. In school, I had been an engaged student and accomplished athlete. As a member of the softball team, I had been hitting home runs and grand slams regularly. That spring, my emotional state consumed me so much that a couple of outfield errors and the worst-timed strike-out left my state-bound softball team at a loss in the qualifying game.

Feeling worthless, I stopped my involvement in all school activities just before my senior year. I became angry, even more confused about life, and out of control.

My only solace was my after-school job. As the oldest child, I often felt I had to protect my younger siblings from the even harsher reality that waited closely on the doorstep of our sheltered life. Even in our younger years, as most first-born children do, I looked after and stood up for them when I wasn't acting as their referee, doing everything I could to be the best big sister because we were a team. I did my share of picking fights, too—but at the end of the day I worried about my brother and sister, hoping for a different world where they would always be happy and safe.

This instinct to take care of people—to turn their difficult days into happy ones—made me a natural at customer service. At the age of 15, I worked at a neighborhood restaurant and loved it. A few months after reaching the long-awaited high school commencement, I got into a relationship with the first guy brazen enough to ask me out. (I am convinced that even in the first moments of our introduction, I could hear nearly every cell in my body screaming to me, *NO! Run now, save yourself!* The message never silenced, and I developed a skill for tuning it out through any means available.) Inside, I was completing a series of transactions —trade offs of what I really wanted for what stood in front of me at the time. Up to that time, it had been my quickest effort to feel as complete and whole of a person in the least number of "moves." The false picture of being "loved" quickly faded as the novelty of having a boyfriend wore off faster than I ever imagined.

He was not very kind to the people we worked with, but even had he been Prince Charming, every moment with him was a degrading slide into an abyss of self-hatred because I knew I wanted a different life for myself. He did, however, introduce me to the idea of opening new stores for our restaurant chain in different parts of the country. I thought *Finally, my escape.*

Fighting Myself and Losing Every Time

The fear of loneliness and the doubt of ever finding anyone else that could truly love me consumed my every thought. I was 18 years old, and measured against my parents' example, I thought I should have had it all figured out. I turned to drinking and seeing other guys while away on business trips in a desperate attempt to numb the agonizing pain I felt, which served to fuel the toxic shame poisoning my once happy and free spirit. Every day was a trade-off for the acceptance and love that I ached for.

On a core level, I didn't deem myself worthy of love anymore, and with each self-sabotaging act, I reinforced a belief of never being good enough. I have vivid memories of lying awake at night telling myself, *It is too late, you have made too many mistakes to turn back—THIS IS WHO YOU ARE NOW.*

Consequently, I isolated myself from everyone, especially from those who truly loved me, including my close friends and family. Without allowing anyone to challenge my depressing thoughts, I assumed a deplorable lead role in my life as my own worst enemy. I did not seek to hurt anyone, yet I became an expert at inflicting my own mental and emotional wounds.

For example, instead of breaking up with my boyfriend, I moved out of state with him. Even after I attempted ending the relationship and moved back to my hometown, I found myself seeking comfort in familiarity—some kind of sense of normalcy—and took him back when he had been fired from the job that led us out of state. A series of unfortunate events led to financial hardship, and I was forced to take a job with a steady salary to support us both.

While I worked ungodly hours to make my small income work, he boasted that his days were filled with job search activity such as interviews with recruiters. For a time we were still doing alright, in spite of both of our poor spending habits, but soon could not afford the lifestyle we had grown accustomed to. I learned later that much of his time was actually spent on adult entertainment websites and gambling—a large portion paid for with my earnings.

I was furious at my situation and how foolish I was for putting myself back into it—except now it was worse than ever. My boyfriend started to become more controlling and violent, and routinely threatened me. Feeling alone, afraid, and on the verge of a nervous breakdown, I found artificial refuge in the arms of a married man. The fabric of my existence nearly unraveled. Anything of value that I ever possessed was traded for the false promises that painted a picture of unconditional love and acceptance. What I found in reality were dull exchanges of mutual pain, a deranged kind of comfort. At least in the shameful exploits I felt somewhat human, alive. My sorrow and grief had company. I didn't have to be ugly alone, and I didn't have to care about the stranger I saw in my reflection every day. *How could I feel so much, yet so much nothing all at once?*

Desperate, and Getting Worse

A little over a year later, I managed to break up with my first boyfriend and break free from my perception of his hold on my life. I submitted my two-week notice at work and enrolled in a couple of classes at a business school.

I thought it was a new beginning—new place, new job, new man —but my previous choices caught up with me. One symptom at a time, my body began to turn against me. Blackouts and syncope, memory loss, severe mood swings including excessive sleeping and waking up exhausted, consecutive days without the ability to sleep, intense muscle twitches and loss of appetite, eventually even suicidal thoughts—it was a new beginning, but the beginning of a downward spiral instead of the bright future I hoped for.

Until the onset of my medical issues I was able to manage the raging anger inside, but this physical pain and the embarrassment from faint-ing episodes was too much to keep bottled up. I lashed out at my new boyfriend on more than one occasion—he thought I was crazy because I had always been such a cheerful, positive girl. A few harsh words and threats of breakup are what prompted me to "get help."

After a battery of tests, including blood draws, CT scans, MRIs, tilt-table tests, x-rays, and a few questionnaires, my doctors wanted to try out an antidepressant to see if it could help minimize my symptoms at the very least. The side effects were just as bad, if not worse. Specialists referred more specialists as my symptoms came on with even greater force and frequency. With one flick of a pharmaceutical promotional pen, the doctor diagnosed me with Bipolar Disorder, and my ability to experi-ence reality was dramatically altered through a higher dosage of a more potent pill.

This pill brought my naturally high energy level so low that I didn't have mood swings anymore. Instead, I hardly had any moods at all! I was simply present, but without personality. I hated how my body felt on this drug, but I figured that it was a small price to pay to save our semi-normal relationship.

Over several years of various pharmaceutical cocktails, I fell deeper into my rabbit hole wallpapered in prescriptions and hospital bills. I was forced to change jobs several times as my "episodes" endangered myself as well as those around me. New symptoms, such as vertigo and debilitating migraines, made it impossible to do simple, everyday activities. I was in a worse physical and mental state than when I first began to seek medical attention.

Stumbling Around in the Dark

About six months into another restaurant job I was assigned a new boss, Sean Murphy. After our first meeting, I knew I would enjoy working with someone so knowledgeable and passionate about the business, and that we could make a fantastic team in working toward improved systems, training staff, and growing the brand.

However, I was concerned that even with my best efforts, I would fail to perform at my personal standards, much less "employment maintenance level," if I didn't start to get well soon. I had already experienced some alarming new symptoms while on the job, and the issues I was able to hide before were becoming significantly more noticeable to my co-workers. Nearly the entire six-month time I reported to Sean, I was certain that I was moments away from termination.

Due to the extreme medication adjustments, much of my memory of this time is slightly fuzzy, yet the guidance that Sean gave to me then will always resonate clearly in my mind. He wisely instructed, "The light at the end of the tunnel is self-lit."

After I put my pride aside and accepted that there was more I could do to course-correct, Sean also reminded me that by focusing on what I could do, that those CAN-DOs would be what would guide me out of my current situation. Much of what he was saying I had heard before in some fashion, but the light bulb finally lit up; not because of the words he said, but the manner in which he approached my situation—as an extremely genuine, caring person.

Instead of treating me like I was a roadblock to his success and handling the situation in a harsh way, Sean reached out as another human being—encouraging me, even expressing belief in me! I had long ago lost any belief in myself, but I thought maybe I could borrow Sean's until I had my own again.

Borrowing Belief, Finding Hope

In regard to my medical issues, Sean reminded me of my voice—that I shouldn't simply accept what one doctor said as an absolute truth, especially when I wasn't getting any better. He pressed the point of not stopping until I got the answers I needed—to persist until I was healthy again.

I could see a giant canyon between where I stood and where I wanted to go; Sean essentially saw my unused bag of equipment, picked it up, and heaved it toward me right at the gut level. He said, "You have what you need—you know how to use it. Now get up and GO! I believe in you, and expect to see you on the other side. You only get to do this life once—why let someone else decide what that is like for you when it is YOUR life?"

I realized I had to take action. I didn't want to be a "quitter," but I surrendered my role in the business and, leaning on Sean's words, prayed for a miracle.

Two days after raising my white flag, I secured a promising job in a different industry, working from a desk as a customer loyalty specialist. There, I could finally focus on reclaiming my health. I could start getting myself out of debt, and begin my climb out of my self-dug hole. This simple job change sparked a tiny belief in the possibilities for my future, and I was determined to work hard. My light at the end of the tunnel was not going to be small. Instead, I was determined to blaze—I wanted to shine like the sun!

Quick success fueled my energy level, and I began to dust off my stacks of sketch pads and notebooks filled with my dreams and ideas to re-imagine my place in the world again. But how was I going to make sure that I didn't go back to that dark place? How could I use my pain to help others out of theirs? Over the previous five years, I had reconnected with family and friends, and this closer support system helped me to see that I didn't have to do this alone—I could be that shining light so others weren't alone either.

To invite people over to my sunny little workspace, I set up a special-ty coffee and tea station on the corner of my desk, which was completely decked out with pictures, inspiring quotes, and on many days, yummy snacks to go with the cheerful conversation. My reputation at work of positivity and fun helped contribute to my success. An increased comfort level in what initially was a foreign industry, and my ability to sell our products by using my good ol' restaurant-grown people skills, had my confidence soaring. At home, my fiancé and I finally started to see some progress in diminishing our financial burdens.

Getting Knocked Back Home

Three months into this hard-working happy life, an accident at my part-time job left me with a neck, back, and abdominal injury. Severe vertigo and migraines returned instantly as I required help with simple tasks—everything from brushing my hair and getting dressed to standing, sit-ting, and even walking. I missed a significant amount of time at work trying to get effective physical therapy, and had to give up the job I loved, since I couldn't perform its duties anymore.

Adding insult to injury, relationship issues caused us to call off our engagement. My step-dad generously offered to let me stay with him and my mom at their house, the home I grew up in. Talk about a bitter pill to swallow! When I first left home as a teenager, I swore to myself that I would never become one of those boomerang kids—no matter what. I told myself that I would rather reside in a cardboard box under a bridge than be a grown adult living in my parents' house. (How can it be that we are so quick to give help to others, yet so resistant to receiving it ourselves?) In the end, I accepted my parents' kind offer.

Now almost six years from the onset of my medical mystery, my con-dition had deteriorated to the point where my vertigo would last for a week or more, and I could not leave that pride-crushing bed in my child-hood bedroom.

I recalled Sean's words and set myself the goal of finding a physician willing to look at all of the data. I found a great doctor, and she encouraged me to take a walk outside every day, even if it was just for a few minutes. Of course I wanted to, but I could barely move my injured body up a staircase, much less go outside for a walk. But I took her advice, and the sporting spirit in me had me challenging myself to go an extra five minutes, or another 20 feet, and then a few more blocks. Inner struggles started to work themselves out as these walks with my beloved dog, Angel, super-charged my healing—and creative inspiration began to surge in my spirit.

A Sunny Outlook at Last

As I healed, I reflected on my life. Even with the progress I had been making, I realized that the root of all of my actions centered on doing what everyone else thought I should do. My life was not aligning with my beliefs. I had become a foreigner to myself, disconnected from my purpose. It is no wonder that I ran out of steam so often, when I was set on the idea of powering through it like a freight train! As emotional and human as we are, we are not designed to handle the roadblocks on life's journey that way. Once I stopped ignoring the cries of my heart and truly LISTENED, things finally started to make sense. I realized that I had been worthy of love all along, but I wasn't giving love to myself. I didn't need someone else to validate me, because I had what I needed inside of me my whole life!

Something amazing happens when you begin to give grace to yourself and make decisions out of love instead of fear. Your ability to understand and forgive expands, and then you are compelled and able to help others in ways you could not before. You walk away from each encounter with a feeling of gratitude for having the opportunity to walk alongside them, and the blessing is, in fact, yours to receive.

As for my physical recovery, the doctor informed me that I was not diabetic, nor epileptic. I was not suffering from a chemical imbalance, or some crazy blood pressure issue. What was really going on was easily treated through a handful of lifestyle changes and chiropractic adjustments.

Off Track to the Right Destination

Just as I was recovering, I reunited with my ex-fiancé. I wanted to give our relationship another chance, and we both believed that our love for one another had not changed. I was not back to work yet from medical leave, but I was determined to move forward despite the chaos. We decided we should just go ahead and get married; and within two months we managed to throw together a wedding on Christmas day.

Before we had broken up the previous summer, we were completely in sync, head over heels in love with each other. But our summer break-up had changed us both. Tying the knot brought a massive implosion over the first and last few months of our short marriage.

The New Year brought a glimmer of hope as I finally filed one of my original business entities with the Secretary of State. Within a month, I also launched my UnDOO dog waste clean-up service, and my confidence reached new heights as each satisfied client referred friends and family. I was almost ready to start the patent-filing process with another idea I wanted to pursue, so I set up phone calls and meetings to learn how I could harness the power of my idea-generating skills. Finally, I had a realistic timetable to create a pipeline of future opportunities.

But even with this success, and even after all of my personal discovery, I slipped back into a few old bad habits. I was doing what everyone else—friends, family, society—said would be right. Even though I had convinced myself it was what I wanted, I knew in my heart that something was just not right. Being married was not a decision I took lightly, but it turned out to be the opposite of what I expected, and nothing of what I hoped for. At just under the four month mark, one argument had me pinned down in our bedroom, unable to breathe, and fearing for my life. I never imagined that at any point I would be calling the police and driving away with my dog.

How did this happen to me? I thought. *This is not how my life was supposed to be!* After a week away, I wanted to do the right thing and felt that I had to give reconciliation another attempt. But I didn't feel safe in my own home, and I constantly had to defend myself and every phone call or email.

On a gut level, I knew what I had to do. Armed with nothing but the support of a few loyal, loving friends, I made the painful decision to leave. In a hurry, I grabbed only the necessities, and pulled out of my driveway for the last time, tears streaming down my face.

Almost immediately after I left, my husband shut off my cell phone and all access to finances. Without access to the resources that would allow me to work my business remotely, I was looking for some type of regular job—anything—to get me in a safe place to survive. A small handful of friends stuck by me, and I traveled lightly: most nights I would stay at a friend's home, but many nights I would sleep in my car to save on fuel if the few odd jobs I took were far away. Up until this point, I couldn't recall a time I felt so pathetic as when I was searching for the spare change I kept in my car so I could buy a small coffee in exchange for use of the shop's WIFI for job applications. What was I, sixteen years old again? I felt beyond humiliated and ashamed.

I filed for a no-contact order for fear my husband would find and hurt me. I did not realize that our county required a court hearing to grant a longer-term no-contact order. I went ahead with the process, believing it would be a simple open and shut case, and showed up to court alone that day, avoiding any eye contact with him as we waited for the judge to arrive. All of the emotional strength I could muster had long vanished by the time the judge finally showed up. I had no idea that my husband could motion for a continuance based on the fact that the attorney he hired was absent on the court date, and we would be working around his availability so it would fit more conveniently into his schedule. He had everything! He was living in our house! He could continue to work! He had all of our money and possessions and had turned my family against me! He physically hurt me! Why were we working around his schedule? I didn't even feel safe in public by myself!

I could not contain the fierce currents of raging terror and anger charging through my body. I became overwhelmed with the feeling he would eventually find me and hurt me again—and he would get away with it, just as he did the night of the attack when he lied to the police. I would be forced to stay on the run and in hiding in order to possibly save my life.

I was so emotionally distraught that the bailiff had to hold me up from under my arms while the court clerk urged the judge that I be given a several minute head start when I exited the courtroom so I didn't have to be in close proximity to my husband. Through my tear-blurred vision I could see the looks of shock and pity from everyone present in court. At that point I didn't care about how I looked to them, or to anyone anymore. I just wanted to be safe, and I wanted to be free from fear.

On the next court date, my husband's attorney suggested that I drop my charges and settle in divorce court. I reminded him that I was only interested in my own safety, but I figured that if he could promise me that his client would stay away from me and my family, stop harassing my friends and clients, then I would go ahead with a swift divorce. My marriage vows were something I took very seriously, but there was no way I would allow that promise to prolong my endangerment.

I was very grateful to accept a position with a restaurant concept I had formerly worked for and loved. This would mean I could finally start to create a plan to come out of the divorce in one piece. During the first several weeks on the job my heart was overjoyed. I was in a place where I was loved and accepted, and I felt like I had somewhere to belong again. A few more weeks passed, and I was given a temporary relocation assignment for work. Given all of the healing I needed in nearly every category of my life at this point, I was excited for a chance to get away from it all and focus on rebuilding.

Saying Goodbye to My Angel

Before I left, I knew that it was finally time for the hardest decision I would have to make yet about one of my dearest loves.

My sweet boxer Angel and I had gotten through tumultuous times together, but it was time for me to stop being so selfish; it was time for me to give up the one thing in my life I had clung onto through everything.

One night, I overheard one of my co-workers talking about how she wanted to get a dog for her family. After a few days, I approached her. I was shocked that she agreed to adopt Angel without having met her, and the night before I left town, I said a very emotional goodbye to my baby girl.

Confident that Angel would love her new family of five kids, and knowing that they would give her the best life in a loving home, I returned inside, soggy red eyes and sobbing, for a meeting with my boss. We were still working out negotiations for my wages in the new role, and I felt at a disadvantage, not to mention embarrassed, being so visibly distraught. I was surprised how caring and supportive he was, and I knew that these next steps on my journey were bringing my life into the right new direction.

Owning My Choices, Healing from Within

After over four months of no contact with my husband, I felt a strong pull to confront my fear, so I sent him an email. *Make decisions out of love, not fear,* I kept repeating to myself. After weeks of conversations, first via email then on the phone, I was ready to see him and begin the process of discussing our divorce in person. This process was extremely painful, and when he asked about what I had been doing with my time away, where I was staying, I shared a little more than I originally had planned to. He reacted with a colorful wheel of emotions, adding that it was my choice to leave and have that struggle.

He was absolutely right.

Despite the difficulties, my mind was clear: I wasn't blaming anyone. I knew that it was going to be difficult for a long time, maybe even longer before I would be back on my feet again. It was my choice; I had chosen to get myself into all of the situations leading up to my choice to leave. It was also my choice every day to get myself into a different, better life.

After experiencing my struggles, and repeated tough lessons, I decided that I would never allow others or circumstance to dictate my life's direction—I was going to be intentional and on purpose, and it was time to live my life on my terms. I was ready to go all in.

The End and the Beginning

We all have unique experiences, yet I believe we all also share a similar thread in the fabric of humanity worldwide—feelings of shame, defeat, loss, unworthiness, heartache, the list goes on. If this is true, if we can share in the perceived negatives of life, I strongly believe that we can also share in the unacknowledged positives that cannot yet be seen. *Love and not fear. Love and not fear.*

> *So here's to a life worth living—a life with no regrets. Here's to the pursuit of becoming who you have always wanted to be. Here's to making choices out of love—abundant love—never fear.*

This was my new mantra. I had come from a place of worrying about everything, to growing my faith that my needs would somehow be taken care of. It seemed strange that as I became more blessed in my life, I felt the worry creeping back into my mind when things were better than they had been in a long time; when for months at a time I didn't know where my next tank of gas would come from.

I had to learn how to have hope of a faith that didn't yet exist in my life, and I had to learn how to not just be confident in my ability to bounce back, but learn how to trust myself to do it. I had to learn to exercise my flimsy muscles of emotional endurance and fortitude. I had to learn how to not give up, no matter how difficult things were.

Start BEEING BLESSED in YOUR Life!

Anyone can change the world right from where they are today—but each of us must wake up to the reality of POSSIBILITY and stop convincing ourselves (or allowing others to convince us) of the converse. **Beeing Blessed** is finding and *creating* joy in our dance of life, despite circumstances.

Consider the honeybee. In a typical working season, its life expectancy is about six weeks. On average during that time, it produces approximately 1/10th of a teaspoon of honey. The honeybee does not sleep, and this tiny insect is vulnerable to many challenges—both in and out of its home. These complex creatures work diligently to seek out and bring nectar and pollen back to the colony. It is not an easy life by any measure, yet the magnitude of their labor extends far beyond the hive, impacting generations of plants, animals, and people through pollination (alongside their other pollinating-species counterparts), accounting for nearly 75% of our global food supply. If a little bee can contribute on that kind of scale, just imagine what we can do if we venture to look beyond our own "neighborhives."

Beeing Intentional in Thought: Ask the Right Questions

Contrary to the natural reaction one may have in a bad situation, the first question one should ask is **not** "WHY?"

Instead, ask "HOW?" How can you learn from this? How will you keep moving forward? How can you use the resources you have, or how can you obtain the resources you need to achieve your goal? How can you be grateful, no matter the situation? How can you pick yourself up every time you get pushed down? How can you help others through their own similar situation? How will you define your success? How can you start feeling successful **right now**?

Now you can ask "WHY?" Why do you want to move yourself forward, why are you motivated to change your situation, why is the ability to make it through worth the struggle?

The answer could be the people in your life relying on you. It could be a lifelong dream, it could be the burning desire for financial freedom, or getting out of a job that you can't stand; it could be health and wellness, freedom to help others and change the world.

What is your own authentic WHY? Clearly define it, SEE IT, and surround yourself with reminders. Your why should be so crystal clear and compelling that even in those inevitable moments of perceived failure you will get up and persevere.

Beeing Bold: Face Your Fear

Just because I am confronting the awkward or scary things in my life, it doesn't mean that it is easy or that I am not afraid. Another tool I created to read aloud when I felt like giving up was like my own personal motivational mantra. Mine went something like this:

> *Fear does not equal defeat. Fear is my built-in mechanism to sound me to initiate action—to light up the switchboard of solutions and ideas. I will not live in fear. I refuse to be a victim. I do not recognize failure in my life. To me, failure is to quit or surrender to life's challenges. The fear, pain, and shame of my past will remain in my past. I do not live there anymore.*

Write your own mantra and keep it somewhere you can read it often. Ask your loved ones to remind you of your mantra when you're feeling down.

Beeing Grateful: Thank Blessings into Your Life

I have decided that no matter what title I hold, I am in the business of making my own sunshine. Wherever I go, I know that I will be successful as long as I keep shining!

When I worked in the customer service job that I enjoyed so much, my medical issues were still in full swing. Knowing in advance that I was susceptible to getting down over my physical pain, and the uncertainty of whether or not I could make the job work out, I made gratitude my game plan. I started by posting the following list of guidelines for my personal work area:

WELCOME TO YOUR SUNNY WORKSPACE!

TODAY is going to be a GREAT DAY—and here are the top 10 reasons HOW YOU will make it so!

10. (As learned from Brandon W. Johnson at the Lifeskills Center for Leadership)
     PLAY HARD! – STAY FOCUSED! – HAVE FUN!
9. Be who you are, don't let anyone or anything drag you down!
8. Keep your priorities straight!
7. No excuses—get it done today!

6. Don't dwell on the past—MAKE THINGS RIGHT!

5. Keep a smile on that beautiful face! Don't listen to any negative self-talk: You are a powerful, creative, and loving presence! You have so much to contribute, even if today it is "only" a positive attitude! Pass it on! Now show those pearly whites!

4. Always be relentlessly learning—you can learn something from everyone!

3. Be bold and confident, yet humble enough to ask for help when you need it! If you fail, learn from your mistakes—sometimes you have to fail big to find your path to success!

2. Leave every situation (and interaction) better than you found it —always add value!

1. Give 100% of yourself 100% of the time—if you aren't "all-in," say NO! It will pay off for you and everyone else too!

Along with these guidelines, I kept an arsenal of other tools nearby to help myself stay on purpose. In my desk were stacks of thank-you cards, and near my computer mouse pad was a running list of "Things I Am Grateful For." It was my personal challenge each day or week to add one more thing to my list of gratitude, and to run out of thank-you stationery before each month's end.

Beeing Generous: Give and BEE BLESSED

We all can be generous, and it doesn't always take money to do so. Share what you *do have* by being your authentic self. Be generous with your time, kindness, encouragement, humor, and spirit of fun. You can be sincere and uplifting with your words. Make it a goal to cheer up that cranky cashier in the checkout lane. Learn how to become the best listener in the lives of those you know. If there is a particular skill set you possess, teach someone who would like to learn from you.

In short, any interaction where you leave someone feeling special, unique, and appreciated is a successful act of generosity!

Beeing Blessed: Feel Blessed by Choice

You may be asking yourself, especially if you are in the middle of tough times, "How do I feel blessed when this is my situation right now?" This is my answer: *don't fake it 'til you make it—choose it 'til you DO it!*

When it comes to feeling blessed in my life, I prefer to not wait. Decide every day that it will be a blessed day, and it will. If we make it a habit to stay positive and hopeful in the midst of painful times, we are able to bounce back much more quickly. It doesn't mean that we are pretending that our situation doesn't hurt, or we aren't acknowledging the wrong or unjust; we are simply choosing that it will not overcome or consume us.

So you say you are in a dark place? Everything you need to get out is already inside of you. Remember: *The light at the end of the tunnel is self-lit. We need to continually ask ourselves: Am I going to be a sunshine maker or a sunshine taker?* You can do this, if you choose to. And you can choose to just get by or get through, or you can choose to *Bee Blessed* every step of the way and beyond. YOU can be that beacon of hope for another, and you don't have to wait until you have reached the other side. Don't you dare give up! *Be as brilliant as the sun,* and keep your radiance rising up with each new day!

Beeing the Sunshine: Live Your Legacy

Our legacies are living all around us: in the lives of those we see on a regular basis and those we unknowingly impact in passing—many of whom we don't even realize are watching. It is our own responsibility (and privilege!) to carry the torch passed from those before us, and to pass the flame on to those around us. Should you choose to accept this challenge, realize that some days you may need to *spark your own flame.* I am honored to cheer you on!

In the wise words of Sean Murphy, "You have what you need—you know how to use it. Now get up and GO! I believe in you, and expect to see you on the other side."

I wish you sunshine on your path, and abundant love in your every thought and interaction. I send you smiles on the faces of strangers, and long-distance hugs to wherever you are on life's journey. May you always bring out the sweetness in others, and know the unique fire and passion that burns brightly in your heart! ▪

 AMANDA M. FERRIS *is a solution-finding entrepreneur from the Minneapolis, Minnesota, area. With a strong influence from personal development books from an early age, she has always been on the lookout for opportunities to add value to the world; through her parents' guidance and encouragement, she was challenged to create and present proposals of her ideas as early as age five. Starting her career assisting in her mother's daycare, she learned how to build curriculum teaching children in a playful, memorable way. Soon after, Mandy worked her way from what began as a summer job at a neighborhood restaurant to over ten years of management, service training, and consulting in the hospitality industry.*

Mandy is known for her high energy and creativity. Her dedication to lifelong learning and the pay-it-forward philosophy truly shines in her training and development programs, and as an alumnus of the program, she also volunteers with BestPrep, a Minnesota-based organization that helps high school students prepare for their future careers and entrepreneurship. Mandy is an intentional creation coach, independent Arbonne consultant, pin-up artist, voice-over talent, and enjoys traveling the world, cooking, and soaking up the outdoors in her free time

Amanda M. Ferris
www.amandaferris.com
mandy@amandamferris.com

7

An Unexpected Blessing
Bradley Howdyshell

We'd been married for twelve years and our life was relatively quiet. My wife Yvonne worked as a public school administrator. I was busy with the management of our funeral homes and "getting the dead where they need to go and the living where they need to be" (Thomas Lynch). The most excitement in our house was the occasional outburst of one of the dogs when they heard the doorbell ring or when one of the ducks from the pond out back came quacking a little too close to the house. This would send the dogs into both hunting and defending mode and create quite a frenzy of escalating violence as one dog tried to out-bark and out-growl the other, often leading to a fight between the two of them...ducks completely unaffected by the drama inside.

Our dinner discussions often focused on the difficulties of being a teacher or principal in public school these days, or on the burdens and responsibilities of caring for the family members of the deceased in our small community. We were two career-minded people who, for the most part, enjoyed our work, challenging as it was, and we had made the decision many years ago to not have children. Little did we know that God had other plans and they would come not in the form of a pregnancy, the anticipation of a new baby and watching him or her grow, but in the form of a troubled nine-year-old boy named Jaylen.

Those dinnertime discussions began to have a different subject during the fall of 2012. Jaylen was often that subject. Yvonne would occasionally discuss a difficult situation she had encountered at school that day, but this one was different. This one broke her heart. She would describe this little boy's personality, charm, intelligence, and amazing potential, all of which were being wasted. He was moving full-steam ahead and, like the Titanic, he was hitting ever-increasing icebergs all along the way—trying to fight and push through on his own. "No nine-year-old should have to deal with the things he has dealt with and live the life he is living," she would say. "I wish there was something we could do for him. Some way to help him."

"Why can't we do something?" I would ask. "Why can't we bring him home from school one evening and just see how things go? Like one of those mentoring programs." My even asking this question was a surprise to me as much as to Yvonne.

As an administrator, Yvonne was concerned with showing favoritism amongst a plethora of students who have just as many struggles and seemingly insurmountable problems at home as Jaylen did. I eventually convinced her to talk to Jaylen's great-grandmother, with whom he was living at the time, to ask if he could come to our home occasionally to get help with homework and spend time with us. An elderly woman with her own struggles and a life of heartache, she agreed.

My mind recalls the uncertainties, on our part just as much as his, of those first few visits to our home. He was clearly nervous—not sure about "going home with the principal"—but he quickly made friends with our dogs and seemed very comfortable with us. He learned to know us in a family setting rather than in a school setting, and we learned to know him as a child needing love and attention rather than another kid...getting into another fight...losing another day of recess. We laugh now, reminiscing that he accomplished the feat of making it through the entire third grade year with hardly any recess.

In learning more of his background from his counselors and social workers we were even more heartbroken. From an early age he had been removed from his mother's home and passed around amongst numerous family members and was in and out of foster homes. He remembers one night as a young boy hearing his cousin being murdered by gunshot outside on the street. He carries scars on his feet from running around barefoot through broken beer bottles, and scars on his legs from untreated insect bites and poor hygiene. As the visits became more frequent, he began to ask if he could spend the night and we happily agreed. For the first time in his life he was experiencing what it's like to have a caring family, and he was loving it!

With a somewhat tenuous realization that she could no longer care for his needs adequately, his great-grandmother agreed to allow him to spend more time at our home, for longer periods, and she eventually asked us to serve as his godparents. Her intention was that he live with us upon her death. His intention was different, He wanted a normal family with a mom and dad—and he wanted it sooner than later. This was something he had never experienced and had a deep longing for. God clearly designed the family unit to include both a father and mother. I think God also gives us a deep, innate longing for His perfect design —even when we can't articulate it.

As Jaylen became more comfortable with us he began reaching out to hold my hand frequently when we were sitting together on the couch or riding in the car. That is one of my favorite moments…when he reaches out and grabs my hand to hold it, simply because he wants to. I cherish that because I know it won't last forever, and he will eventually hold my hand only if he has to, not because he wants to.

It's amazing when I think how quickly he developed a trust in us and wanted us to be his permanent family. This has not come without struggles, though. We shared his desire to be his family and it became more and more evident that remaining with his aging great-grandmother was not the best scenario for him or for her. Others in his biological family expressed interest but this came to no avail. We had concerns about sending him back into the type of situation from which he was removed. There were several very intense court appearances where the judge heard from all parties and eventually made a final ruling as to where

Jaylen should live. In our last court appearance we were granted full custody and Jaylen has been living with us full-time since. As he continued to let his guard down, our names bounced back and forth from Mr. and Mrs. Howdyshell...to Bradley and Yvonne...or sometimes a jumbled up combination as he worked through that in his mind. Now there is no more confusion or uncertainty in what to call us. He eventually decided to make a final transition from Bradley and Yvonne...to Mom and Dad. Words we never thought we'd hear.

Although hearing him call me Dad and seeing how far he has come garners feelings of satisfaction, my proudest moment as "Dad" and the most important moment of triumph in his young life was, and always will be, an April Sunday morning in 2013. It was Easter Sunday and we'd just heard a powerful message from one of our favorite pastors, Dr. Robert Jeffress of the First Baptist Church in Dallas, Texas. During the time of decision, Jaylen raised his hand indicating his desire to become a Christian. With one arm around his shoulders and the other holding his small hand, I was privileged to lead him in a prayer of invitation to meet Jesus Christ and accept Him as the Savior and Lord of his life. I remember so clearly his tender yet decisive words as he asked God to forgive his sins and to come into his life and to change him. No matter how many successes and how many failures I experience in helping to raise him and to shape his future, my greatest journey with him began that day and will continue forever—teaching him about God's love, forgiveness, acceptance and healing. Then teaching him to share that message with others.

When I think of where he is now in relation to where he has come from, it's truly amazing! During his early visits to our home, it was heartbreaking to see his filthy clothes and the obvious fact that he had not bathed in...well...who knows how long. It was a challenge, but we were eventually able to get him to take a bath and change into clean clothes while at our home. Although he fought it hard, upon doing so it was evident that he felt so much better—not just physically but mentally. I think this is a perfect picture of how God works in the spiritual part of our lives. We fight against Him and what He wants to do in us and through us.

Like Jaylen, we all need rescuing! When we allow God in, He picks us up, washes us clean, changes our hearts, the entire course of our lives, and, most important, our eternal destination.

Jaylen is enrolled at Fork Union Military Academy, a college prep school as opposed to a hard-core military prep school. It was founded by a Baptist minister and continues to operate from its Christian roots. Being a part of this school has impacted his life tremendously, and he is receiving a great education, being involved in sports, chapel and Bible study. No longer is he wearing those filthy clothes but is looking sharp and clean in his dress uniforms and battle jacket.

Our journey has allowed us to share some amazing experiences with him. I recall a trip to a conference in Dallas where we often meet with a wonderful community of small business owners from around the world. We decided to take Jaylen, not only to experience his first trip on an airplane and his first trip out of the state of Virginia, but also to experience the teachings of some wonderful people like the legendary Zig Ziglar, an incredible mentor, teacher and man of faith. One evening of the conference is always dedicated to sharing struggles and needs with one another and then praying together. Jaylen's sensitivity has always astonished me and it was demonstrated clearly to all those in our small group that night. As needs were shared and tears were shed, he was connecting with each person and the challenges they were facing. When we prayed for one another, Jaylen surprised us all by praying aloud in front of total strangers, petitioning God on their behalf. I'm certain that many of the tears shed around our table that night were because of the simple beauty and purity of a sweet boy asking God to "help Mrs. S. and her children not to be sad since her husband left home" and to "help Grandma feel better" and "help us all to have a great rest of the day."

He also learned many lessons at the conference, as evidenced the following Sunday at church. After lunch we returned to the church to change clothes and found the automatic revolving door had been turned off. As he was struggling to get the door to turn, I said, "I think it's locked, Bud, you'll have to come around and go through the regular door." He continued and was able to get through the door and met me in the lob-by, proclaiming, "It's not locked, Dad, I just had to push harder to reach my goal!"What a great lesson from the mouth of a child. No matter what challenges are in front of us, if we push long enough and hard enough we can reach our ultimate goal. Zig would be proud.

In a recent conversation between Jaylen and me, he provided a perfect summary of how to be a dad and lead a home."I'm proud of you, son."

"I'm proud of you too, dad."

"Why?"

"Because of the way you lead our family."

"How do I do that?"

"With love, and discipline, and laughter."

My daily prayer is that God will give me the wisdom (James 1:5) to always lead our family and our business with those three things at the forefront. Love, discipline and laughter. Over the past couple of years, Jaylen has proven to be a happy, funny, sweet and caring boy—all those things that were buried deep down inside and had been crushed by the dire circumstances under which so many children live. It's sad and scary to think where he would be right now if God had not allowed our paths to cross and given us a willingness to "do something" for him. I'm still in awe when I think of the work God did in my heart to even consider get-ting involved, and giving me not only a desire but also a determination to "do something."What began as an occasional visit to mentor a student in trouble has turned into a wonderful—unlikely—unexpected family!

There are countless children, and not just in third-world countries, but maybe just down the street or even right next door, who need some love and attention. If we don't reach them, especially with God's love and sacrifice while they are young, they will most often remain lost. Will you ask yourself how you can "do something" to help even just one? What a difference it could make! ■

 BRADLEY HOWDYSHELL. *Bradley was born in Staunton, Virginia, and grew up in Augusta County. He and his wife, Yvonne, own and operate Thacker Brothers Funeral Homes with locations in Scottsville and Lake Monticello, Virginia. They also own and operate Charleston Candle Works based in Charleston, South Carolina. In addition to involvement at church, Bradley has served on the boards of community organizations such as the Foundation of the Frontier Culture Museum, Staunton and Fluvanna Rotary Clubs, Staunton Performing Arts Center, Augusta County Historical Society and the Shenandoah Valley Funeral Directors Association. He enjoys music, singing, gardening and history.*

Bradley Howdyshell
Thacker Brothers Funeral Homes
PO Box 185
Scottsville, VA 24590
434-953-7890

Charleston Candle Works
PO Box 80622
Charleston, SC 29416
434-953-7890
www.charlestoncandleworks.com

8

Truths About The Boogeyman

Barry R. Jones, Jr.

We all know the story and we have all seen him up close and scary. Yes, it was the boogeyman. He is in the closet; no, wait, he is behind the dresser; no, no, under the bed. He must disappear in the light.

Please leave the light on—please, please—in case he comes again!

He is a mythical, mystical creature that lurks around the room in various hiding places, scratching at the windows, opening drawers, moving through the shadows. The best history I can find on boogeyman is uncertainty of when the tales first came about. Some say the tales date to the 16th century while others say it was 1836 when it was used as a term for the devil. However, the word might come from the middle English word bugge, which means: frightening spectre. Similar words around the world are bogge, boggart, bogy, and bugbear, which are ghosts or frightening creatures.

The boogeyman is universal and there are different versions all over the world.

In many Latin countries he is called the Sack Man—a monster with a sack that carries naughty children away.

In Afghanistan he is called Bala, which means monster person, used to make children go to sleep or take medicine.

In Belize he is called Tata Duende, which is the protector of the forest animals and was used to keep children in at night.

In Bulgaria he is called Talasam, who raids during the night, taking kids who misbehave, and in Harry Potter's version he is a shape-shifter —he would take the shape of someone's fears.

Here in the Deep South of the United States we call him the Booger Monster, which we use as a threat for everything we want our kids to do or not do with the threat,"The Booger Monster is going to get you."

Details are kind of sketchy, but apparently he has no particular size and a shape that changes, and his aura is amorphous. No one knows if it is male or female, no one really knows what he looks like, but the one thing that is common is he is the most terrifying creature to have ever lived inside their minds.

We all live with our version of the boogeyman every day. He is the monster that sits up on our shoulder and whispers in our ear,"you can't do that, you might get hurt, you're not good enough to do that, those days are over, it can't be done," and every other self-defeating thought we have. Sometimes we let him win just because we sense the shadow of him in our mind. Unless we learn to live with him.

Truth # 1 He Disappears in the Light

My story of the boogeyman is lifelong. He started out as a technique used by my uncle, who was only a few years older than me, trying to get me to behave and go to sleep at night. So he passed down the story of the monster that comes and gets little boys who do not go to sleep at night, who go out in the road, and other things he wanted me to do or not do. Then, one night I was all alone in the room with the lights off and he showed up because I did not go to sleep. At first, he was just a whiff of light, and then he was hiding behind the dresser, lying in wait for me., I screamed, "Maw Maw, HELP! HELP! He is going to get me!" and my grandmother came in and said,"Who is going to get you?"and I said, "The Booger Man! He is behind the dresser!"So she turned on the light and POOF! He was gone.

When we first see or hear the boogeyman he fills us with self-limiting beliefs, doubt and fear. He wants us to accept this as truth and real without any proof. When we turn on the lights we find he is just like our childhood Boogeyman, he is not real. It is just fear:

False

Evidence

Appearing

Real

So the best thing to do when we do experience the fear of Boogeyman thoughts is turn on the lights and watch him disappear. When we acknowledge we do have fear by bringing those thoughts out in the light, usually we find they are just not real or even scary.

> *The only thing we have to fear is fear itself.*
> Franklin D. Roosevelt

When my son was five years old he wanted roller blades, so I got him all the pads to go with them—wrist, knee, elbow—and a helmet. Got him all geared and ready to go and he stood there like a statue. I told him to give it a go. He said,"No, dad, I am scared."I said, "Scared of what, son?" He said,"Falling."So, knowing he was covered from head to toe in pads, I assisted him in falling and laughing a few times until he realized that the fear was not real. You see, by bringing that fear into the light he realized his protective gear was going to keep him safe and he could just have fun.

There are thoughts we have every day that if we just bring them into the light, we find that there is no danger and we could actually enjoy doing whatever it is that he is telling us we cannot do.

I think the best way to do this is to picture the situation in our head and push the picture out into full light, inspect the scene and run through the different scenarios that could take place, just to see if there is even anything to worry about and if what the boogeyman is saying is even close to being true. Or is it just a self-limiting belief trying to scare us from our dreams?

Truth #2 It's Just Dirty Laundry

Sometimes just turning the lights on is not enough for us to believe he is not there. We still feel he may be hiding under the bed. Boogeyman thoughts can cause hardening of the attitudes that can even cause the NOTS.

> We can **Not**
> We dare **Not**
> We should **Not**
> We would **Not**
> We could **Not**
> We have **Not**

In order to get rid of the NOTS, we have to convince ourselves that the boogeyman is a liar, and change the thoughts he has given us. So we need to look under the bed in our mind and see that the only thing that is under there is just dirty laundry.

Dirty laundry is the stuff from our past we have messed up or failed at and we keep it hidden under the bed. All it does is stink up our thinking and the boogeyman uses these thoughts to make us believe that is the way it will always be.

> *Successful people maintain a positive focus in life no matter what is going on around them. They stay focused on their past successes rather than their past failures, and on the next action steps they need to take to get them closer to the fulfillment of their goals rather than all the other distractions that life presents to them.*
>
> Jack Canfield

For instance, when I was in my early twenties I had tried taking a few college courses and it just did not work out, so I was under the belief that because I could not make it in college and barely made it through high school I would never be a big success. One day I was talking to my best friend and sales manager about it, and he told me I was smelling and believing my own dirty laundry. He then asked me, "What do you consider your best accomplishments in life?" I told him I was an Eagle Scout when I was a Boy Scout, and I made it through Marine Corp boot camp. So he said, "You know how to be successful, and that is a resource you can pull from. Instead of focusing on the failures, focus on the successes." He said, "Energy goes where your focus goes, so focus on the fact that you know how to be successful." He then told me that if I put as much time and effort into learning how to sell as people put into getting a degree, that I would make a considerably larger income than most of them and it would be skills that are used in every career, because every product and service has to be sold. So I took his advice and studied everything from A to *Ziglar on Selling*, attitudes and business, and he was one hundred percent right. Within two years I was a sales manager making double the income a twenty-four-year-old male makes even by today's standards, and have carried those skills and attitudes forward into every business I have successfully owned, giving me the ability to be 100% debt-free in my early forties with enough savings to seventy-five percent retire and just travel for awhile.

Had my friend not helped me understand that it was just dirty laundry under the bed, my thoughts about failing might have come true and I would still be struggling as I was when I was 22.

The best way I have found to deal with him is every time I feel that the boogeyman might be under the bed I look and see if it is just dirty laundry. We all have to realize yes, you have failed at things in the past, but you have also succeeded. So celebrate your past successes and know you have the resources to push forward, immersing your time and efforts into the new task. And you will succeed.

Truth # 3 It Will Not Kill You

The boogeyman would have you believe that he walks with us, silently shouting compelling orders. Compelling because the orders are life-changing, life-controlling, and life-disturbing to us. He gets us caught up in a sea of turbulence, thinking there is no way out and no way to succeed. We have to take control of our thoughts by figuring out what is really worst-case scenario. Once you do, you will figure out that it will not kill you. You realize it is usually not even a quarter as bad as you built it up in your mind to be.

Learn to see things as they really are, not as we imagine they are.
Vernon Howard

Immediately after serving in the US Marines, where I always had three hots and a cot (three meals and a place to sleep), I had no clue as to what I was going to do, but I did know my tour was up and it was time for me to get into the real world. I was thinking that I might end up on the streets of Los Angeles, begging for money like some of the Vietnam veterans I had seen there. Well, after a closer look, I realized I could sleep in my car for awhile, take a shower at the gym with my membership, get a job and find a roommate. That's just what I did for a few months. Looking back, it was the best learning experience of my life and it gave me a reason to get my life together. It did not kill me, either. Once I figured out it was the only option I had, it was not so bad. It was not as comfortable as I had wished it would be, but I made it through and it made me stronger. If we deal with our worst-case scenarios then we have no choice but to make it better and it will not kill us.

The best way to do this is look at the situation in our mind as if we are giving advice to someone else. You see other people's problems and have an easy solution, but yours are hard.

Truth #4 He Can Be Your Friend

Once you have figured out worst-case scenario and accepted it, you can then move on to making him a friend through positive expectance of the situation. He might be a friend who argues back at first, but if you keep telling him how it is going to work out just right he will eventually believe you and start helping you make it turn out right.

Visualize this thing that you want, see it, feel it, believe in it. Make your mental blueprint, and begin to build.
Robert Collier

When I quit my job and started my first business, the boogeyman was telling me, "You will have to go and beg for your job back within three months." But I did not. I figured out what type of income I needed to survive and figured out what it would take to do those minimums and set goals for where I wanted my business to be in three years. Then I created a picture of what that would look like in my mind and held it there on a constant basis until the boogeyman agreed and started pushing me in the right direction. And many successful businesses later I have not gone to beg for that job back.

The process for doing this is:

Set a written goal;

Create a bright, clear, crisp picture in your mind of achieving that goal and hold it there until it is done.

The boogeyman will always be trying to force thoughts in your mind which just are not true. Remember these truths about him and you will learn to live peacefully with him.

BARRY R. JONES, JR. *is a serial entrepreneur, speaker, coach, adventurer and hypnotist. He is a licensed skydiver, scuba instructor, rescue rappeller and a certified executive fire walk instructor. He is also a Ziglar Legacy Certified trainer and certified John Maxwell founding member, speaker and coach. Barry's mission is to help others grow and achieve their definition of living life to the fullest.*

Barry R. Jones, Jr.
www.foundationaltraininginstitute.com
foundationaltraining@outlook.com

When He Shows Up, Things Happen
God works in mysterious ways
Mike Koehler

G rowing up if you were to tell me that God was looking down on me with favor or I was blessed, I would have probably not understood what you were talking about. As I reflect back over my life, I realize that God has had plans for my life all along. Some may choose to call it all coincidence, but I choose to believe things happen as part of God's master plan. I still wonder what **His** assignment is for me, but I take the opportunities **He** gives me in preparation and grow.

> *"For I know the plans I have for you," declares the LORD, "plans to prosper you and not to harm you, plans to give you hope and a future."*
>
> *Jeremiah 29:11 (NIV)*

I was raised in a middle-class blue-collar family in the suburbs of Detroit, Michigan. I was fortunate to be the oldest of three kids in our family. We were not an overly religious family by any means and, in retrospect, we were probably a little under-religious. We were practicing Catholics and attended Mass most weekends with our mother, although we would sneak out after communion to beat the traffic. I don't remember my father going to any masses other than when one of us kids was receiving the sacraments. As matter of fact, my first Bible was given to us

as a wedding present and, even though I had attended catechism classes for six or seven years and received the sacraments of Baptism, First
Communion, Reconciliation, Conformation, and Marriage, I knew very
little about Jesus and God and even less about the Bible. How would one
know what God had planned for them if they did not know God?

*"For we are God's MASTERPIECE. He has created us anew
in Christ Jesus, so we can do the good things He planned for
us long ago."*

Ephesians 2:10 (NIV)

As a youngster, I was never a social butterfly, more likely being de-
scribed as an introvert or being a shy child, although I did have a unique
set of gifts where I related to numbers and understood complex math
formulas from a young age. I also had an obsession with figuring out
how mechanical things worked. In today's world I would have been a
nerd. My parents tried to get me interested in sports; I had no natural gifting, which was a shame because I was always the tallest kid in
the class. Academically I excelled in all my classes with the exception of
physical education. I was never popular and had very few friends, but
never really noticed because I was busy figuring out how mechanical
things worked. I would sit in my bedroom and draw blueprints for a
hobby. The family moved when I was in seventh grade. There wasn't
trauma or drama because I did not have any close relationships

"Blessed are the meek, for they shall inherit the earth."

Mathew 5:5 NIV

Having entrepreneurial parents, they gave me a lot of responsibility
at a young age so I learned the value of work ethic, diligence, and determination, which God has used to create success for me throughout my
life. My high school years were typical for an introvert, taking AP college
classes and working two part-time jobs. I was an honor student with
straight "A's" but not involved in any extracurricular school activities. I
had a hard time fitting in and making friends, but I did have the respect

of my peers because of my academic ability, which I found comfort in. I was looking forward to heading off to college and becoming an engineer when my parents decided it was a good idea for me to take vocational machine shop in my senior year instead of AP college classes. Imagine being that shy, introverted kid who was used to and comfortable with the people in his classes and where his future was headed, then everything is turned upside down. Now I would need to meet new people and those people were not academics, they were typically people who did not care about their grades or the future; basically, they were ones who needed to take a vocational class. *How depressing! How confusing! Why? How could my parents do this to me?* were all questions that ran through my mind. I became depressed and buried myself in my new major and my part-time jobs.

In retrospect, this was the point when God stepped in because **He** had answers to all those questions, yet I could not see them. What would have happened if I had gone to college to become an engineer? How different would life be? When I think about it, I was introduced to my future wife via a blind date through a friend I meet at the vocational school. The direction God created for me and the opportunities that **He** orchestrated are amazing and nothing short of miracles.

> *"Do not be conformed to this world, but be transformed by the renewal of your mind, that by testing you may discern what is the will of God, what is good and acceptable and perfect."*
>
> Romans 12:2 (NIV)

In 1982, the metro Detroit area was in a major recession where there were thousands of tool and die workers laid off and here I was taking vocational machine shop. How bright of a future was that going to be? Vocational machine shop was not a challenge at all because it was all based on simple mathematics, so everything came very easily and I was able to excel. Because of my performance, I was given a co-op job at a local tool and die shop, so now I could hide my depression by burying myself in three part-time jobs and school. Having been raised with a strong work ethic and being academically gifted created opportunities at that shop to advance at a rapid pace. **He** showed up and things started to happen. I got trained on CNC (computer numerical control) equipment, ran CNC equipment on a second shift, became foreman on second shift, got trained on EDM (electrical discharge machining) equipment, got promoted to a department head, ran the largest department in the plant, and was promoted to plant manager in six short years.

The tool and die industry being a transient industry, a former employee called with a job offer running CNC and EDM equipment that would increase my income by about $10,000 a year. At that shop I was able to learn how to design with CAD (computer aided design) and work on developing prototype parts and machines for the auto industry. Out of the blue, another door opened with an opportunity to use my new CAD experience, my manufacturing experience, and my machine development experience. I got hired to be a design checker so I was checking engineers' work and designing the same machines that the engineers did. What a roundabout way to end up an engineer! Amazingly, **He** showed up and things started to happen.

> *"Ask and it will be given to you; seek and you will find; knock and the door will be opened to you."*
> *Mathew 7:7 (NIV)*

Something was stirring inside of me, as I would see the sales guys going through their routines, and I knew that was what I needed to do. The problem was, you could not get a sales job without sales experience, yet you could not get sales experience without a sales job—which was a kind of catch-22. I was always a good student so I bought some books and tapes on goals, selling, and self-development and began learning what it took to be in sales. Being diligent and preparing pays dividends when **He** opens a door for you. Early one evening there was a knock at our front door and it was a financial salesman trying to set an appointment. For some reason, I set an appointment for him to come back and make a presentation. A week later, the financial salesman showed up and presented some financial concepts, except he was not good at presenting, so we endured two hours of boredom. The highlight at the end of his presentation was when he asked, "Have you ever thought of doing something part-time or making a career change?" I thought, *Is he really going to give me a chance to get sales experience without giving up the security of my full-time job?* That first year I got all my licenses, learned a bunch, made a few bucks, was named "rookie of the year" and gained confidence, which helped me start to overcome being an introvert. My second year I had the confidence to make a change and that set **His** plans into motion.

> *"The Spirit of the LORD will come powerfully upon you, and you will prophesy with them; and you will be changed into a different person."*
>
> *1 Samuel 10:6 (NIV)*

Helping people became my passion, so after two years part-time then two years full-time, **He** laid upon me the desire to relocate. I had the confidence, work ethic, and determination to relocate where **He** wanted me to grow, so we moved to Columbus, Ohio, from the Metro Detroit area. We did not know anybody in Columbus, so we started out cold and had to network, which would have been very hard for the introvert that I used to be. We started to develop a strong team and grow a business. Four months later, I was promoted to Vice President and six months after that I was awarded my "Financial Independence Console" ring for breaking the $100,000 in income mark. **He** showed up and things started to happen.

I found that I really enjoyed training and developing leaders. I had developed a training system that produced results and worked with all types of people. I had a unique leadership style and created a fun work environment so we continued to grow. I also adopted the Zig Ziglar concept of "You can have everything in life you want if you will just help enough other people get what they want," and our business had exponential growth. Wanting to give back, I got involved with the Big Brothers and Big Sisters organization and began serving on the condo association board. **He** looked down on us with favor and the business continued to grow. Awards, recognition, trips, money and the good life were all rewards for work ethic, diligence and determination. Then **He** blessed us with the biggest gift of all when, after thirteen years of marriage, our daughter was born.

He opened more doors and I was able to use my leadership skills to give back to the community by serving on the Finance Committee at church, Chairing Parish Console, and being on the board of the United Way. Business was growing and life was good.

> *"The thief comes only to steal and kill and destroy."*
> *John 10:10 (NIV)*

The perfect storm began when our very spiritual priest, for whom I had a great respect and was a good mentor, was replaced by a young MBA priest that I did not enjoy working with on the committees and consoles that I served on, so I stopped participating in church. Our business had grown so fast that I allowed people to work in my business who lacked integrity and they were affecting the environment and morale. A former associate violated his contractual agreements by stealing clients and recruiting current associates out of our business. The financial industry was changing. At the same time there were people who owed me money who were not paying their bills. We had issues with our tenants in our rentals. The economy was hitting rough times and being in a financial business during them was taxing. The Devil showed up. The combination of all this wore me out so I stepped back. I found out that without my day-to-day leadership things got worse. It was no fun. I needed a change, but what was the right change?

> *"But for those who are self-seeking and who reject the truth and follow evil, there will be wrath and anger."*
> *Romans 2:8 (NIV)*

I chose to pursue a dream of NASCAR racing—not as a driver but as a crewmember. I landed a gig in Nashville as an engineer on a NASCAR

Busch team. Nashville was six hours south of my home and family in Ohio. Some would believe that **He** had made this happen, but really it was the opposite. The racing industry was very physically demanding and I was unable to find peace mentally. It did not take long to figure out this was not the right direction for me, which then had me second-guessing my life and questioning the future. I began having feelings of emptiness and indecisiveness, which was not like me. I was making this change to be happy but that was not what was happening because I was missing some key elements in my life. Hope for the future was disappearing and things looked bleak. The economy continued to falter, further reducing my investment portfolio and my residual income.

I had received an invitation to a non-denominational church for a service; after attending, I felt different, like hope was coming back. As I was traveling to races for the next few weeks and not attending services, that feeling faded. I was excited to get back early from a race and go to church. I was headed to service when my pick-up truck was involved in a horrific accident where the driver's door was broadsided by a truck traveling 60-plus miles per hour. Somebody did not want me to go to service. After the accident, I sat alone in my apartment, contemplating my life, the decisions I had made, and what I was going to do. I realized that I should have been killed or at least severely injured in that accident, and I received only a baseball-sized bruise under my arm. I prayed for direction. I made some decisions on where I wanted to go and the people I wanted to have in my life.

"The righteous choose their friends carefully, but the way of the wicked leads them astray."

Proverbs 12:26 (NIV)

The next day I made one call to someone I had met at the track who owned a race team and a race car parts warehouse near my house in Ohio. Amazingly, I got hired to sell race car parts at a decent rate of pay and the promise of an opportunity for ownership. To my surprise, I was the only one there with a real sales background and I was able to excel.

I was really starting to enjoy life again. I had a great thing going; I got to spend time with the family, I got to go to the track and sell parts, I had a job that was challenging, I had hope for the future, but I was still missing something. I had not been to church since I left Nashville. **He** was working in my life, but I was still distant and there were still things in my life that were not working.

My daughter Jessica was playing on a kindergarten basketball league at her school when a fellow dad who was sitting next to me suggested that she should play in the Upward Sports league. It made sense for her to play basketball in the winter because she played soccer in the spring and fall. We signed her up, not knowing much about the league other than it was hosted in a local church. I took Jessica to the first practice with a team that consisted of eight kindergarten girls and one coach, so, in other words, mass chaos. I volunteered to help out and the next thing you know I am officially an assistant coach. The Upward Sports program is a Christian-based sports ministry so part of practice is a Bible verse and a small Bible study. It is hard to ignore God and **His** works when you have to answer eight kindergarteners' questions about God during practice. The next thing you know, I was the head coach the next season and dealing with the parents' questions, too. Do you think **He** knew I would draw closer because of Upward Basketball?

> *"But seek first his kingdom and his righteousness, and all these things will be given to you as well."*
> *Matthew 6:33 (NIV)*

Still I had not made it to a church service since I left Nashville, but **He** was going to fix that. I got home from work to find an invitation to a Marriage Makeover at a local church but I did not give it much thought at the time. Amazingly, that invitation kept showing up and hung around for the next three weeks, so we registered. What is the possibility of finding a church with a prayerful pastor with a powerful message who used to sell financial services? I would venture to say that the odds would be pretty slim unless it was part of **His** plan. We showed up for the Marriage Makeover, related to the pastor's background, understood the message, and found a new church. I went from not going to church to not missing a service. We were learning about the Word, taking notes, and we could not get enough. The teaching of the pastors was incredible and so applicable. The next thing you know, I was helping start the Upward Basketball League at the church, teaching a Life Group, and even hosting a car show at the church. You have to believe that **He** had this in **His** plan for me.

There are always peaks and valleys in life. While my relationship with **Him** was the best it's ever been, the economy was tough on the racing industry so the company I was working for was losing money. The owner offered me an opportunity to purchase the company but the price was way too high for a company that was losing money. When we could not come to terms he let me go with no real notice. For the first time in my life I was unemployed, so what did **He** have in mind for me? I had faith something would show up, so I diligently sent out resumes. I got a few interviews here and there but nothing that was a fit. It was weird, because everything I felt good about did not call back, and everything that I thought was horrible did call back. One day I interviewed at an auto repair shop that was dirty, grungy, and ugly, so when my wife asked how it went I told her it was a dirty, grungy, and ugly auto shop and I really did not want to take the offer they made me. As we sat in service that week, the pastor's message was on opportunity. He said, "Sometimes the opportunities God lays out for us are dirty, grungy, and ugly." So I took the job. I learned how to write service orders, learned about auto repair, and learned how to use a diagnostic scanner. I knew that **He** had to have a plan because this shop was disgustingly dirty and frustrating to run.

Going to a non-denominational church gives you a different perspective on religion. I realized that my passion for helping people and my ability to train people were not being used in my Nascar job, my race parts sales job, or this service writer job, but I was to have faith that **He** has a plan. I had ministry service laid on my heart, but more than just leading a Bible study. I met a Chaplain from Racers for Christ at a car show and swapped stories of **His** works in our lives. For the next month I could not shake this feeling and **His** call to action. I went through the process to get ordained as a Chaplain with the Racers for Christ organization. Imagine: I get to share my faith, use all my skills, and help people while at the race track! That was definitely part of **His** plan, and as a side benefit I get to work under the track Chaplain who is an awesome man of God. I think I have been a help to him, but he has been an incredible influence in my faith walk and become a great friend.

> *"The soul of the sluggard craves and gets nothing, while the soul of the diligent is richly supplied."*
>
> *Proverbs 13:4 (NIV)*

I had been diligent in my service at the auto repair shop by learning some new things and helping them grow. I got a call from the largest tool company in the world to set up a series of interviews. I was being interviewed for a diagnostic sales position which involved selling diagnostic scanners and service writing software that I had been using at the auto repair shop. I had used it every day, so I had experience and I was knowledgeable about the equipment and programs. Do you think this was in **His** plans for me? Once I was past the phone interview process it was time for a face-to-face live interview. I had spent twenty-five years doing face-to-face sales, so what could go wrong? The Devil steps in with an attack—a heart attack—they were calling to set up the interview as I was on my way into the hospital. I set the interview and **He** made sure everything worked out so I could be there. They hired me and the duties were similar to what I did in the beginning of my financial services career. The sales process is a little different, it is a lot more corporate, and positive recognition is less than abundant, but all and all it is a good fit for me. I apply the principle of "You can have everything in life you want if you will just help enough other people get what they want," and provide first-class customer service. It took a little time, but it started to pay dividends; I was recognized for top sale-to-forecast. I was awarded "Diagnostic Sales Developer of the Year" in my second year with the company. I felt like I have a great fit, I really know the product, and I get to work with great people. **He** showed up and things happened.

I had gotten out some of my old motivational materials and listened to a set of CDs on goals by Zig Ziglar. I had something laid on my heart similar to what I had with Racers for Christ, but it did not make any sense. I struggled to figure out what it meant because I did subscribe to the Ziglar emails, both on sales and on faith, but I was baffled. I did know I owed Zig a debt of gratitude for teaching me the principles that allowed my career to take off in the early years and were still paying dividends today. I did know that I needed my batteries recharged because I was running on empty and missing passion for what I did. The real question is, what did **He** have planned?

The Ziglar Legacy Certification was everywhere I turned. It was on my Facebook, in my email, there were prerecorded podcasts, live podcasts—so was this a sign? It was already the end of October and the program was in about three weeks near Dallas, Texas. I did have unused vacation time that I did not plan on using, and the money for the program was in my checking account in the bank. I made the trip contingent on air fare and hotel cost and I got amazing low air fares and a relatively low hotel cost but they gave triple points that took me over their platinum level for the year. **He** showed up again and things happened.

It was an amazing week that I cannot begin to describe. The Ziglars, the staff, my classmates, the environment, **His** presence—just amazing. I had not felt this positive and emotional in ten years. I was excited about being excited again.

Not to make a long story even longer, but all this being said, the real question is why?

I do not know what God has planned for the rest of my life, but I do know that it will involve the passions and resources **He** has given me. God has a plan for all of us. He knows that we cannot do our assignment on our own so **He** prepares for bigger things by giving us smaller things first. **He** gives us blessings with the responsibility to use them the way **He** would. **He** wants you to win and be successful. I can only hope that my story so far provides you with encouragement and hope to work through the hard times and show you the glory of God in the good times.

"I can do all things through Christ who strengthens me."
Philippians 3:14 NIV

If you have never given your heart to God or recognized Jesus as your Savior, now is a good time to pray about it.

In your personal faith journey, I suggest you find a good Bible-believing church and attend regularly, find a local Bible study and learn about God's promises, and dedicate your work to the Lord.

"Commit to the Lord whatever you do, and He will establish your plans."
Proverbs 3:14 NIV

 MIKE KOEHLER, *throughout his career, has had a passion for personal development and a talent for leadership that has allowed him to grow into high level positions. Over the last 25 years, he has studied leadership, entrepreneurship, and business development and finance, which has allowed him to help grow and develop leaders for several large companies. Now Mike has a passion to help others learn the same principles and motivate and inspire them to achieve their goals and dreams.*

Mike is a passionate, yet personable, speaker/trainer/coach who is capable of engaging audiences of all sizes and appealing to a large demographic. His passion for helping people shines through in everything he does. His message is a simple one of hope and prosperity through knowledge and training.

Mike Koehler lives in a rural suburb just north of Columbus, Ohio, with his lovely wife of 28 years, Rhonda, and their teenage daughter, Jessica. In addition to being a dedicated husband and father, he maintains strong community ties. Mike is employed by Snap-On Tools as a Diagnostic Sales Developer and is a Ziglar Legacy Certified Trainer for Ziglar, Inc. In addition, he owns Results by Mike, a company that does training, coaching and motivation. He currently is working towards his MBA at Mount Vernon Nazarene University. He also serves as the Associate Track Chaplain for Racers for Christ at National Trails Dragway.

Mike Koehler currently holds licenses for life, health, and property and casualty insurance in the states of Ohio and Michigan. He also holds a series 6, 26, 63, and 65, with FINRA for investments. Mike has certification from the ASE (Automotive Service Excellence) for Levels C1 and P2.

In the past, Mike Koehler served as a Regional Vice President for Primerica, which was a member of Citi Group; General Manager for S&V Automotive, running Truechoice Motorsports, PAP Parts and Pipercross USA; and as a crew member for Day Racing Enterprises.

You can get more information about Mike at:
Resultsbymike.com

Additional information can be found at:
Ziglarcertified.com/mikekoehler
www.facebook.com/resultsbymike

You can contact Mike at:
Phone 614-581-7701
Mike@resultsbymike.com
resultsbymike@gmail.com

Follow Mike on:
Twitter @resultsbymike
Instagram @resultsbymike
www.facebook.com/resultsbymike

10

Just Say YES!
Patricia Morris

Sitting in my therapist's office, I hear the words, "We need to discover what is missing in your life." *Missing? There was nothing missing,* I thought; my life was perfect. I have the most wonderful and loving husband, two beautiful and healthy kids, a great software sales job with the best boss, a best friend who was always there for me. Everything on the outside seemed perfect, but I was dying on the inside. I would cry in the arms of my husband every night. Depression was crushing my heart. One particularly dark day, one of my friends said, "You need an encounter with God!"

"An encounter with God, what does that look like?" I responded. I grew up Catholic in Brazil, attending a private Catholic school, doing all the rituals and saying all the prayers and had never encountered God. *I don't think that is possible,* I thought. But I was desperate for something good, for a change.

On a Friday night I joined a Church retreat. With my arms crossed I was thinking, *What am I doing here?"* By Saturday morning my heart had started to soften. I heard incredible testimonies of how God had touched people's lives and they were forever changed. I was starting to feel hope. The entire day was filled with powerful moments of truth and revelation. For the first time, I was studying the Bible and the Scriptures were leaping from the page, touching my heart. That evening I was asked to make a list of all the sins I could remember I had committed. That was a humbling and overwhelming exercise. It definitely showed me how desperately I needed saving. After writing the list, I had a moment with God, acknowledged that I am a sinner and asked for His forgiveness. I burned the list in the campfire and never again felt shame.

That evening, when the invitation was made to accept Jesus Christ as my Lord and Savior, I stood up proudly. My friends were crying and I didn't really understand why. The next morning at breakfast, a gentleman congratulated me for the decision I had made the night before. I defensively replied, saying that I always knew who Jesus was. His response was so wise that I will never forget, "You are missing the point. It is not about knowing who Jesus is, but accepting what He did for you." Things were starting to make sense to me.

On Sunday, we were learning about the Holy Spirit and the power that He offers us. As I studied about the baptism of the Holy Spirit, I became convinced that this was what I needed for my life to change. It came time to end the retreat with worship. For the first time, I worshiped God from my heart, not reciting prayers I had memorized. All of a sudden, I heard a heavenly language that I had never heard before and I opened my eyes. I saw a pastor praying with a lady and she was speaking in the most beautiful language I had ever heard. I wanted that blessing for me! Another lady who had been negative the entire weekend was going to say something about what was happening, but I didn't want to hear it. I stopped her three times by saying "I don't want to hear it, I want that blessing for me."

As soon as the pastor finished praying with the lady, I grabbed him and said, "I want that blessing for me, will you help me?" He asked me to keep repeating "I glorify the name of Jesus." So I did. All of a sudden, I felt the most amazing tingling all over my body, my tongue got thick, and even though I was still saying "I glorify the name of Jesus," the words that were coming out of my mouth were not that. It was the most amazing experience I ever had. It only lasted a few minutes, but it was powerful enough to change my life. I immediately ran to my friends saying,

"I had an encounter with God!!!"

I called my husband to let him know that I had felt the presence of God and that I was a different person. He never expected me to have changed that much. I called my mom to ask her for forgiveness and to tell her that I forgive her. That evening, the pastor asked me to share with the congregation my testimony. I just remember saying, "I'm going back home to McKinney and I will start something. I don't know what it is, but I will start something." I saw my therapist the following week and thanked him for his services. I told him, "I found what was missing in my life, and His name is Jesus Christ!" He thought I had lost it and needed more therapy. I insisted that I was good and didn't need any more treatment. He asked me to give him a call when I came down from my "pink cloud." I never again felt hopelessness, that hole in my soul had been filled with the most amazing joy. I was on fire for the Lord, there is no other way to describe it.

I remember praying on my way to work, "God, you have saved me, given me eternal life and set me free. What can I do for you? I want to be your hands and feet on this earth." After one month of praying this prayer, my pastor at the time, Doak Taylor at Lifepointe Fellowship, challenged the congregation, asking what kind of life do we want to live; do we want to live a life just about us, or do we want to serve the community? I wanted to serve the community. I am embarrassed to say that I had lived in McKinney for seven years and had no idea there was a homeless shelter in my hometown. At my Church small group, we were discussing ways we could serve the community as a group. One of the ladies shared an idea she had of doing a party in a bag that we could take to the children at the shelter. When she said that, a flood of memories came racing through my mind, reminding me of my birthday parties as a child in Brazil.

My parents got divorced when I was five and my mom, sister and I moved six hours away from my dad. In order to provide for my sister and me, my mom traveled six months out of the year selling semi-precious stones all over the world. But she always came back in town for our birthdays, organized these amazing, elaborate parties, and allowed my dad, who would drive six hours, to stay in our apartment with us. On my birthday my family was united, I felt loved, special, important, protected and celebrated. At this time God said to me, "That's how I want these children to feel on their birthday." God used my past to birth in me a passion and desire to celebrate the uncelebrated and share with them the love of Jesus.

I couldn't stop thinking about that; all I wanted to do was throw birthday parties for homeless children. I contacted the homeless shelter and they welcomed the idea. The friend who invited me to the Church retreat that changed my life advised me to start a non-profit organization and create a logo. My response was, "I have no idea how to start a non-profit or design a logo, all I want to do is celebrate kids." My friend offered to design the logo and three days later he delivered what is now the Birthday Blessing logo. The next Sunday, an elder of the Church who had heard of my idea approached me, offering to do all the paperwork for starting the non-profit. The paperwork was completed and paid for… Birthday Blessing was officially a non-profit organization. Someone else from the Church offered to host the parties at the place where he managed, Peter Piper Pizza, the coolest place in town. I jumped with excitement, thinking how awesome it would be to get the families out of the shelter and celebrate them at a fun place. One day, Susie Jennings, the founder of Operation Care International, came to our Church to share her testimony and what God was doing through her ministry. I was so inspired by her that I asked her to become my ministry mentor.

I got a call from the Samaritan Inn letting me know that a single mom with two boys had just moved into the shelter and the boys' birthdays were March 8 and 9. I will never forget meeting Rose, Mason and Jaden. You could tell that Rose was tired. Her car had broken down, then she lost her job, and was later evicted from her apartment. It is hard looking for a job without transportation. The birthday boys were Mason who was turning 10, and Jaden who was turning 2, in March of 2009. I asked Mason what he wanted for his birthday and what his clothes sizes were. I shared with him that his party would be at Peter Piper Pizza and he responded by saying, "No way, I have been dying to go there!" I said, "You can invite three friends and there will be games, gifts, pizza and lots of fun." You could tell he was happy. I asked him, "Mason, do you know who is giving you this party?" He responded, "Mrs., Mrs." I think he was trying to think of my name. I said "Mason, it is not a Mrs., but God who is giving you this party. He loves you and celebrates you, which is why He wants you to have an awesome birthday party." A couple weeks later at his party, he and his friends had a blast. After opening all his gifts, which said "To: Mason, Love, Jesus," Mason raised his hands and said, "Thank you, God!" At that moment I knew I wanted to do this for the rest of my life. Birthday Blessing connects children to God, it makes Him real to them.

The day that I went to meet Rose, Mason and Jaden at the shelter, there was a Channel 8 news van parked in front. I poked my head inside the van and asked them what they were doing. They were covering a story about how the faces of the Samaritan Inn were changing. People that never expected to be homeless now didn't have a way out. This was during the recession in 2009. I told the reporter about the first Birthday Blessing party that would be taking place Sunday, March 22nd. He said he didn't work on Sundays so I gave him my card and asked if he would see if someone else at the station could come out. I followed up with an email to the station, but never heard back. Ten minutes before the party started, Channel 8 news came in with microphones and cameras. I was completely surprised and unprepared. The reporter interviewed me and some of the guests. That night, I watched the report and was stunned with what I heard me saying. What I said was something I had never thought or dreamed about. I said, "My vision is to have a branch of Birthday Blessing all over the world so that every child can be celebrated." That was a big vision. I felt God say in my heart, "That is my vision." Three days later, I got a call from Good Morning America wanting to feature Birthday Blessing on their show. Hearing Diane Sawyer say my name was surreal. About one hundred people contacted me. Twenty-five people from different states were wanting to start a branch of Birthday Blessing in their town, people wanting to get involved and donate services. I was overwhelmed by the response. I had just thrown one birthday party, I had no idea how to expand. This showed me the potential of this ministry and how it touches people's hearts.

Birthday Blessing is now six years old and we have celebrated more than 700 children. We have expanded to Dallas, Seagoville, Fort Worth and Brazil. Birthday Blessing has a team of volunteers who are passionate to make a difference in the lives of children who are going through a lot of uncertainty and difficulties. Our goal is to make the children feel loved, important and celebrated. We tell them that God loves them and celebrates them. We organize birthday parties once a month at each location to celebrate the children who have a birthday that month. Each birthday child receives three gifts from their wish list, clothes, shoes and a Bible. The children can invite their families plus three friends. The parties are a lot of fun and the children always have a great time. At the end of the party we share the gospel of Jesus Christ and give the children the opportunity to accept Him as their Lord and Savior. Children are ready for something good, they are looking for hope. At every party we have several children stand up and come forth to pray, giving their lives to Jesus. We now have a discipleship program to walk alongside these children, mentoring them and showing them the love of God.

With the ministry growing, and more lives being celebrated, I started to think about doing full-time ministry. I was no longer passionate about selling software, I was passionate about celebrating the uncelebrated. But I had a really good job, making good money. At the time, my income was 50% of my family's income. My husband was getting his MBA at SMU and had a bright career in front of him. We agreed that when his salary equaled what we were making together, then I could quit my job and dedicate myself to full-time ministry. As my husband was promoted and received pay increases, I would let go of some sales territory, going part-time. The timing of everything was so perfect that within two years his pay doubled and I quit my job. Looking back, I can see God's hand guiding us through every step of the way.

My life has purpose now. To make a difference in children's lives is priceless. Looking back at this journey, it is encouraging to know that I don't have to have it all figured out. I just have to take one step at a time and trust the Lord to lead me. When God put this ministry idea in my heart, I could have come up with all kinds of excuses not to do it: I work full time, have two little kids, I don't have much Bible knowledge, someone else is better qualified, etc. But God doesn't call the equipped, He equips the called. All I had to do was say YES. Who would have thought that in six years I would be attending seminary school and doing full-time ministry? I am a firm believer that with God all things are possible.

Dare to be a difference maker... just say yes. ■

 PATRICIA MORRIS *is the founder of Birthday Blessing, a ministry that organizes birthday parties for children living in poverty. Within six years of existence, Birthday Blessing has celebrated more than 700 children in the DFW Metroplex and in Brazil. Growing up in Brazil, where everything is an excuse to party, Patricia's mom would organize elaborate birthday parties to celebrate her special day, not knowing that one day that tradition would turn into a ministry.*

After getting her business degree from UTD, Patricia went to work for a Dallas-based software company where she quickly became the top salesperson. Twelve years later she traded her career to pursue full-time ministry and obtain a Master's Degree in Practical Theology from King University.

Patricia enjoys spending time with her husband and two daughters—on the beach whenever possible.

Patricia Morris
patricia@birthdayblessingministries.org

11

The Five Action Steps Of Leadership—
Becoming A Sheepdog
Richard Morris

What is a sheepdog? My good friend, Lt. Col. Dave Grossman, retired Army ranger and WestPoint psychology professor, shares the following warrior maxim he gleaned from a Vietnam veteran, an old retired colonel:

> Most of the people in our society are *sheep*. Sheep account for about ninety-eight percent of our citizens. They are kind, gentle, productive creatures and generally hurt one another only by accident. Then about one percent of our citizens are the wolves and the wolves feed on the sheep without mercy! Do you believe there are wolves in the land? You had better believe it! Then the final one percent of our citizens are the *sheepdogs*, who live to protect the flock and confront the wolf. If you have no capacity for violence, then you are a healthy productive citizen—a *sheep*. If you have a capacity for violence and no empathy for your fellow citizens, then you have defined an aggressive sociopath—a *wolf*. But what if you have a capacity for violence and a deep love for your fellow citizens? Then you have a *sheepdog*, a warrior, someone who is walking the hero's path. The sheep generally do not like the sheepdog. He looks a lot like the wolf. He has fangs

and the capacity for violence. The difference, though, is that the sheepdog must not, cannot, and will not harm the sheep. Still, the sheepdog disturbs the sheep. He is a constant reminder that there are wolves in the land.

We are all born as *sheep*. As babies and small children, we are totally dependent upon others to survive. The role models we have can lead us to continue as *sheep*, become *wolves*, or become a *sheepdog*. Civilization, as we know it, would not exist like it does today without sheepdogs to protect the sheep and hunt the wolf.

My Journey—Becoming a Sheepdog

My dad was a remarkable man and a warrior—a *sheepdog*. He was a professional boxer before he entered WWII. During the war, Dad was a tank commander in the 759th Battalion for General Patton's Third Army. Dad drove the tank that Patton would often ride in, leading the charge. Dad also spent time in the 82nd Airborne and was at Pointe Du Hoc at the Invasion of Normandy. He was a celebrated war hero with many medals and commendations. Dad was also the kindest, most encouraging, and most humble man that I have ever known. While I began as a *sheep*, Dad raised me to become a *sheepdog*. Starting when I was about five years old, Dad taught me how to box and some Jiu-Jitsu that he learned in the Army. He was training me in the way of the warrior—to be a *sheepdog*.

God has given me positive role models who were sheepdogs and godly men: Dad was the first; he taught me with *faith, hope,* and *love*. Dad loved me unconditionally and he had faith in me before I ever had faith in myself. He had hope that I would one day become strong enough to protect myself and others. Dad told me that it is my responsibility to keep the Morris name honorable; never to bring shame to the Morris name. Dad taught me that I should protect the weak from bullies. This sacrificial love was demonstrated to me and soon defined my role in society.

When I started taking karate in February 1971, I was the youngest in my classes. I was fourteen years old, stood 5'3" tall and weighed about

135 lbs. Paul Smith, in my introductory lesson, asked me how far in karate I wanted to go.

I asked, "What is the highest belt?"

He responded, "Black belt."

I then asked him if there was a higher-ranking belt than black belt and he said, "Theoretically, 10th degree black belt is the highest, but there are none of them today."

I told him, "Then I will be a 10th degree black belt!" I saw him roll his eyes and smile; Paul was only a brown belt himself. I believe that the reason I was willing to reach for the top is because Dad taught me how to believe in myself. I went home that night with the belt test requirements up to black belt and I marked the calendar with the soonest date that I could test for each belt. Even then, I understood the importance of writing down my goals in order to achieve them.

It would take me three years if I were to test every time I was allowed. I practically lived at the karate studio. I cleaned the mat and bathrooms daily, because I understood that it would build discipline and character. I missed my first belt test, because we did not have the five dollars for the test fee. Belt tests were only given bi-monthly. That location closed in June, so I started training with Pat Burleson, the chief instructor, at his main location.

On November 16, 1971, while in the advanced karate class, I was beaten badly during sparring by an adult national champion black belt. Karate was much rougher then, but this was too much! I was a 15-year-old blue belt. That night, I drove my motorcycle home and told Dad that I wanted to quit karate. Dad listened intently as I told him what happened, and he could see that I had a broken nose, two black eyes, and bruised ribs. Dad said that he was going to talk to Pat Burleson the next day about what happened; he was going to confront him for his letting a grown man fight me so hard.

As we walked in the next day, Mr. Burleson said, "Richard, I wondered what happened to you—you never miss helping me teach the kid's classes!"

I told him that I was quitting karate. He looked puzzled. Dad told Mr. Burleson that he needed to speak with him right away. Mr. Burleson looked at me and said, "Richard, if you will teach this class while I talk to your dad, I will get back with you in just a few minutes."

I was concerned about how the conversation was going, but I was excited to be teaching the kid's karate class by myself. About 30 minutes later, Mr. Burleson stepped outside of his office, stopped the class and asked me, "Richard, how do you like teaching class?"

I said, "I love it!"

Mr. Burleson then asked the class, "Did you like Richard teaching this class?"

They all said, "Yes, sir!"

Mr. Burleson then looked at me and said, "Richard, would you like to be the new teacher for this class?"

I said, "Yes, sir!"

Mr. Burleson then told the class they would now address me as "Mr. Morris," as I was now their teacher. Somehow, I forgot about the broken nose, black eyes, and bruised ribs. I became a teacher that day and I have never missed even one week of training or teaching since November 17, 1971. I learned perseverance and the discipline of responsibility. I noticed the students who would miss one week, and allow that one week to turn into two. Eventually, the students would quit coming to class. For me, quitting was not an option, so I promised myself that I would never miss even one week. I was promoted to black belt exactly three years and two months after starting karate—at least two years faster than most of the students who made black belt; less than one in one thousand of the students who begin karate ever make it to black belt. My goal setting and determination did pay off!

For years, I wondered what Dad said to Mr. Burleson. After Dad's death in 1992, Mr. Burleson told me what really happened in his office that day: "Your dad sat in my office and drank coffee with me. He told me, 'I don't mind Richard fighting hard and know that injuries are just part of being trained as a fighter, but the older black belts need more control until Richard gets older and stronger.' I told him that I agreed with him and would make sure it didn't happen again. After talking about unrelated things for some time, your dad told me, 'Mr. Burleson, I want you to make a man out of my son!'"

Dad wanted me to be a *sheepdog*.

Karate was a major transforming process in my life. I have been very successful as a fighter and teacher. I've taught more then 100,000 students since I began teaching in 1971 and have had the opportunity to inspire and build strong character skills in my students. I was very shy as a teenager, and Mr. Burleson would take me to help with seminars until I was confident to lead seminars on my own. He said that it would give me confidence to speak in front of others. It paid off: over the years, I have taught self-defense seminars internationally to tens of thousands of people. I am also one of Pat Burleson's first students to promote to 10th degree black belt in both American Karate and Tae-Kwon-do. My first karate teacher, Paul Smith, is still a brown belt to the best of my knowledge.

Because I was a black belt, when I turned eighteen I got a job as a bouncer in a popular teenage hangout near Texas Christian University. There, I met many Fort Worth police officers who became my friends and several became my students. I accompanied some of the officers on ride-ins and found it to be exhilarating. It gave me a chance to see how police officers can truly help people within the community. I also loved the warrior lifestyle! My role as a sheepdog continued to develop. I joined the Fort Worth Police Department and began the police academy in January 1978, just two months after I got married. Since then I have served in many roles, finally retiring in 2014 as the Gang Intelligence Sergeant, after 36 years of police work. As a retired sergeant, I continue working with the police department as part of the Critical Incident Stress Debriefing Team, the Peer Support Team, and as a volunteer chaplain.

In 1982, I opened my first karate studio and taught classes during my off-duty hours. My studio became successful, giving me the avenue to teach and motivate others. In 1985, a student of mine asked me if I had ever heard of Zig Ziglar. I had not, so he loaned me two Zig Ziglar cassette tapes. Within one month I noticed that my attitude was more positive and my business more profitable! Soon, I met Zig at a seminar in Dallas. He was humble, genuine, and thoughtful. Zig made me feel as if I was the only other person in the room. I met his son Tom Ziglar in 1985 and we have been friends ever since. Tom first invited me to give my Christian testimony that same year during the Monday morning devotional time at the Zig Ziglar Corporation. Zig was such an encourager; he became my friend, karate student, and my personal mentor. Zig said he was my "Dutch uncle." I instructed karate classes at the Zig Ziglar Corporation for about four months in 1985.

Over the course of my police career, I taught self-defense programs for children, women, and senior citizens. Each of these endeavors brought the Fort Worth Police Department positive national media attention with Ted Koppel at *ABC Nightline*, Peter Jennings at *World News Tonight*, CNN, and many more.

Karate paved the way for me to become a police officer. I have taught self-defense and arrest control tactics to thousands of police officers, federal agents, and those in the military. I am a sheepdog who trains sheepdogs!

Do You Want to Become a Sheepdog?

Remember that about 98% of people are classified as *sheep*. Not all of my friends are *sheepdogs*; I love sheep and I have dedicated my life to protecting the sheep and hunting the wolf! One of my friends noticed that the people that I spend most of my time with are sheepdogs, such as Lt. Col. Dave Grossman, as well as my martial artists, police, military, and spiritual warrior friends. He said, "Richard, I have noticed that you collect warriors." He is right! I also train them to deepen their skills.

While not everyone aspires to be a sheepdog, few initially set out to become a wolf. But, if you do want to move towards the warrior's path of becoming a sheepdog, here is the formula:

1. LOOK for Sheepdogs

We must actively look for sheepdogs to emulate, instead of waiting for them to enter our lives by chance. We all experience transforming events; and even when we are unaware, we can find mentors who can help to transform us into who we want to become. These events and the mentors we follow will be either positive or negative. We must gravitate toward the positive and stay away from the negative. In order for us to succeed, we need to follow those whom God brings into our lives for His purposes. Negative people can be an anchor in your life, holding you back from achieving excellence. You have to make a decision now to gravitate towards the positive role models.

"Surround yourself with the dreamers and the doers and thinkers, but, most of all, surround yourself with those who see greatness within you, even when you don't see it in yourself" (Zig Ziglar). God instructs us to claim strength, even before there is evidence of that strength:"...let the weak say,'I am a warrior.'" (Joel 3:10, ESV)

You may say,"This is good for you, but I didn't have a positive relationship with my father or any of my teachers." I want you to consider that you can find sheepdogs all around you, such as your coworkers, neighbors, family members and more. You can go to your library and check out good books on those men and women who have the sheepdog mentality. You might have to get out of your comfort zone, but it will be worth it! Learn more about your family members and their faith, hope, and love. Watch shows like *Blue Bloods*, *Rifleman*, and others where the heroes are positive. Ask yourself what causes these heroes to "tick"? Study your Bible and you will see that the Bible heroes were warriors—sheepdogs.

Many of us grow up with low self-esteem, and we all need others in whom we can trust. We may not yet have faith in ourselves, but we can learn to trust and have faith in those who love us. I am talking today about finding positive and *trustworthy* mentors whom we can model our life after. We must seek and follow those people who are wise and who have good character; who inspire us to succeed. For me there were many, all godly people: Dad, Mom, Mr. A.D. Pickett (my wood shop teacher), Pat Burleson (my karate teacher), Becky (my wife), Lowe

Leach (my father-in-law), Inez Leach (my mother-in-law), Rev. Bob
Weathers (my pastor for many years), Zig Ziglar, Merle A. Wang and Curtis
Brannan (my best friends), and many more men and women that I con-
tinue to study and admire.

2. LISTEN to Your Sheepdogs

Once you find sheepdogs, learn from them. Pay attention to the positive qualities of the righteous sheepdogs. Make it a daily discipline to
read and learn from them.

"Finally, brothers, whatever is true, whatever is honorable, whatever
is just, whatever is pure, whatever is lovely, whatever is commendable, if
there is any excellence, if there is anything worthy of praise, think about
these things." (*Philippians 4:8*)

3. LEARN From Your Sheepdogs

There are many lessons you can learn from these sheepdogs if you
pay attention. Start with those who demonstrate determination, discipline, time-management, a strong work ethic, and strong family values.
Identify and study the qualities that you want for yourself and seek a
sheepdog with those qualities. The best way to learn is with your own
embodiment of these qualities.

4. LIVE Like a Sheepdog

Imitate your sheepdogs' behavior. Zig Ziglar said, "It is better to imitate excellence, than to create mediocrity." After you identify righteous
men and women sheepdogs, imitate their positive qualities as you develop your own.

"Brothers, join in imitating me, and keep your eyes on those who
walk according to the example you have in us." (*Philippians 3:17*)

"What you have learned and received and heard and seen in me—
practice these things, and the God of peace will be with you." (*Philippians 4:9*)

Notice that Paul said we are to follow the example and practice!

5. LEAVE a Sheepdog Legacy

What do you want your grandchildren to remember about you when you are gone? Define what you want to pass forward to future generations, as well as to those who will study your sheepdog behavior. When you teach others the valuable lessons you have learned, this is when the fun begins! "True joy comes when you inspire, encourage, and guide someone else on a path that benefits him or her." (Zig Ziglar)

Share your faith with those whom you love. "Christ Jesus, and what you have heard from me in the presence of many witnesses entrust to faithful men who will be able to teach others also." (*2 Timothy 2:2*)

In conclusion, remember that not every sheepdog is a physical warrior like a George Washington, General George S. Patton, or Chris Kyle; many are warriors in their faith or determination for social justice such as Mother Teresa, Billy Graham, Franklin Graham, Rosa Parks, Zig Ziglar, and many more. Search them out, follow their guidance, and, as you learn from them, live accordingly. You will leave a sheepdog legacy that will far outlast your years on this earth! ■

 RICHARD MORRIS *is President/CEO of Richard Morris Seminars.*

Richard retired as the Gang Intelligence Sergeant in 2014 after 36 years with the Fort Worth Police Department. Richard is a volunteer police chaplain, Peer Team and Critical Incident Stress Management Member for the Fort Worth Police Department.

Richard is a 10th degree black belt in Tae-kwon-do and America Karate. Having taught Karate since 1971, Richard has affiliate schools worldwide. He teaches the psychology and physiology of fighting, but the physiologic principles also apply to the activities of daily living (ADLs) to prevent Worker's Compensation injuries in the workplace. Richard, also an inventor, has a team of scientists that evaluate how people get injured in fighting and doing ADLs, so that the risks can be minimized. This team of scientists consists of psychologists, medical doctors, sports physiologists, physical therapists, kinesiologists, mathematicians, engineers, an OSHA trainer, police officers, military Special Forces Operators, and more.

As a published author, he is currently writing a book, On Fighting, with renowned military and police trainer, Lt. Col. Dave Grossman (ret). The On Fighting Manual, a companion book, is expected to be out by May 2015. Motivated to Live *and other books are currently in the works.*

Richard's karate student Tom Ziglar appointed Richard to be the Exclusive Personal Safety Coach for the Zig Ziglar Corporation. Richard is an internationally acclaimed speaker and is a Certified Ziglar Legacy Speaker, Trainer, Consultant, and Coach.

As a former United Methodist pastor, Richard understands fully the importance of inspiration, as well as motivation. Richard and his wife Becky have been married since 1977. They have two adult children, also advanced black belts: Jacob and Michelle, and a granddaughter, Chloe.

For information on having Richard speak to or train your organization, please call or e-mail him today!

Richard Morris Seminars
PO Box 12162
Fort Worth, TX 76110
Office: (817) 921.2399
Cell: (817) 999.8208

Richard@RichardMorrisSeminars.com
www.RichardMorrisSeminars.com

12

It's In The Cards!

James Packard

Growing up I always wondered whom I would marry. What would she look like? How would I meet her? That question was answered when Sherry walked into Mario's Pizza Parlor that June day of 1968 in Boothbay Harbor, Maine. It actually was love at first sight. I'm pleased to say that I found the right one the first time.

It's been forty-five years and it gets better every day. Sherry has been by my side and very supportive in every venture that I've been involved with.

Now that I'm sixty-five, I look back and wonder if my life mattered. Did I do what God intended me to do with my life? As I'm typing this story, I'm hoping that He's not done with me yet; I hope that this isn't the final chapter, lol!

The last ten years of my life, I've been involved in a greeting card company. How I got there and the signs that directed me there will, I hope, make for interesting reading or, better yet, make you reflect back to see if there are any signs in your past. As I write this story, I'm going to refer to those signs as "God winks," for I really do believe that God has been directing my life. I wish that I could remember where I first heard those words, "God winks," but I can't.

As I look back at my current adventure, I'm feeling better about where I am and what I'm doing because God provided me with little signs for years—I just didn't recognize them as signs. I'm beginning to wonder how many signs I missed over the years.

For the better part of my working career, I was an entrepreneur and businessman. I started out as a sales rep working for a large copier company and eventually started my own business. I started with $500.00, a Volkswagen Beetle, a son less than two months old, and a very supportive wife.

When I was forty-nine, I sold our company to a Fortune 500 company by the name of Ikon Office Solutions. My goal was to sell before my 50th birthday and I accomplished that with 30 days to spare. It's amazing the power of goal setting, but that's another chapter for another day.

I would be remiss if I didn't mention one thing about goal setting, which involved my kids. My kids would always come to me at Christmas and say, "Dad, what do you want for Christmas?"

I didn't need any more ties nor did I want them to spend their money, so I asked them to put their goals in writing. We decided to list things that they wanted to accomplish in the coming year. We selected four categories that first year....family goals (be nice to your mom, dad, brother, dog, etc.), sports goals (which team did you want to make), physical goals and, oh yes, my wife stressed academic goals. That exercise, which we continued throughout their junior high school, high school and college days, proved to be one of the best gifts that I ever gave to my sons—or them to me, for that matter. Those goal sheets are among my most prized possessions.

As I mentioned earlier, we sold our company to Ikon. We were one of approximately 80 of the largest copier dealers that they purchased in a five-year period. We were told that our company was ranked among the top two or three companies on how we ran and managed our business.

One of the things that we required of our salespeople was to have monthly contact with every client.

I learned early on that the number one reason why your customers leave you is because they feel you took their business for granted. The second reason was because they simply forgot about you.

I also knew that for every month when you don't have contact with your client, you actually lose 10% of your influence.

I was not going to allow that to happen, so I required our sales reps to have monthly contact with their customer base. I didn't care if it was through a phone call, a visit, or a card...they just needed to communicate. It proved very successful, for we eventually had close to a 40% market share with major accounts in our state...thus one of the reasons that we got bought out!

I always remembered how we could never really find any good sales-oriented greeting cards in the marketplace. We could find cards that said "thanks," but nothing really eye-catching. I stored that memory in the back of my mind.

When I retired and moved to Arizona, I realized that I needed to do something. My golf game wasn't good enough that I even wanted to play every day and, although my wife loved me, she really didn't want me around the house every day, either!

So I started a greeting card company (it seemed like a good idea at the time)...making greeting cards for businesses. The concept was well received, I could count people like Tom Hopkins, Harvey Mackay and Zig Ziglar as customers. I was having some fun, using my creativity but not making much money. I began to realize that although the concept was well received...the actual sending of cards was easier said than done.

As my wife would say, you're right back in the rat race. I was coming up with a lot of the ideas. I was financing the cards being printed, I was warehousing the cards, doing the purchasing of the envelopes, doing the fulfillment, overseeing the sales, collecting the money, etc.

The most rewarding part of this new business was working with my sons, Jeff and Adam. I got to realize how talented they were and how they were light years ahead of most people their age. I'm convinced it had a lot to do with their goal setting skills. They were both working with me part-time. I believe they got a better appreciation for what it's like to work in the business sector as entrepreneurs...a great foundation for what was to come later down the road.

Here comes into play what I call one of my first "God Winks."

On January 15, 2005, while in my office organizing some of my file folders, I came across one of Jeff's goal sheets. These are the goals/action sheets that we've been using for years. Jeff said that he wanted to pray more often, which I found pretty interesting, for it wasn't really something that I did on a regular basis. I occasionally prayed for the safety of our family, but I didn't really pray for guidance from a business perspective. Well, that night as I was lying in bed, I remembered Jeff's goal of praying more often for guidance so I decided to give it a try.

I said, "God, as You know, I don't pray a lot for guidance in business. I do occasionally ask You to keep my family safe but I don't really want to bother You about business stuff because I can only imagine how busy You must be with more important matters." That night I figured that maybe I had earned the right to ask for some business-related advice, since we had never really discussed business matters before…so I asked for guidance. "Am I doing what I'm supposed to be doing? Should I even be in the greeting card business? I do have some options You know. Do me a favor; somehow let me know that You're listening to me tonight. I can see the water feature from my bedroom window, so perhaps You could make a bird fly down into the water feature. Better yet, show me a shooting star… something, some type of sign that we're communicating."

Well, nothing happened, there was no sign and I fell asleep.

At 4:10 AM on January 16th I woke up out of a sound sleep with the following message. I heard God say something to the effect of, "Send out the cards for your clients." I thought, Yes! What a brilliant idea! I would send out the cards for my clients. I would offer that as a service. I got up, walked to my den, and wrote that idea in my journal. I also jotted how thankful I was that God answered my prayer.

God knew that I was struggling with my card business. He knew that people loved my cards, bought them, but the business wasn't going like I wanted it to. People bought my cards but they didn't send them out as much as they or we thought they should…it just wasn't convenient and cost-effective for them to do so. A card is a personal thing, it's an impulse buy, and if you don't have the correct message then it doesn't get bought, let alone sent. He's telling me to send out the cards for my clients. He wanted me to offer a follow-up system for my clients! He understood how hard it was for me to keep in touch with my clients, so what a great service for me to offer to others. By offering a service to my present clients…it would give me residual income and my clients would be thrilled with such a service. I started to calculate…if one of my clients created 50 new customers per month and we sent out a five-card campaign (for which I would charge $29.95), we would make 50 x $29.95 per client x 12 months per year). We could have a great little business!

I went to one of my best customers that morning to run my new concept by him. He loved the idea. He would start by giving me 75 customers' names and I would create a five-card campaign. I billed him $2446.25 and I set up his campaign with his approval. It was a little tricky figuring out how I was going to send cards 2, 3 , 4 and 5, but I worked it out.

The second month that I was supposed to pick up another 50 or so new clients didn't go as smoothly. The end of the month came and went, and I received only about a dozen names—and that happened only about 20 days into the month and after four visits and numerous phone calls…what a hassle! You can imagine what a nightmare it was, trying to set up a few more accounts (manually, I might add) to their slowly-growing list. A lot of their addresses were incorrect, which didn't help as well. As I picked up a few additional accounts, things were getting more and more complicated, so I hired a lady to handle the scheduling of mailings. That helped a great deal, but what a hassle to coordinate and sell.

I was having all of the challenges that came with a traditional business. There was the challenge of creating new cards, printing, inventory, accounts payable, accounts receivable, warehousing, fulfillment, employees, negotiating meetings, and, of course, creating new clients while maintaining good customer follow-up. I was doing it and not really enjoying it, but that was what I was directed to do by GOD—or so I thought. It was a rough period of time.

On May 16th, I got a call from Jeff asking me if I wanted to meet with a man named Jerry Haines. He was a promoter for Jim Rohn and they were having an event in town on June 15th. Jeff thought if we played our "cards" right that we could have a sponsor's table at the event....maybe we could sell a lot of our greeting cards there. He asked me if I wanted to meet with Jerry at El Paso BBQ and discuss the idea.

We met on May 17th at 3:00 in the afternoon (on my mom's birthday). As we talked about the Jim Rohn event (Jeff and Adam's favorite speaker), it became clear that I wasn't going to ask Jerry for a table because during that conversation, we found out that one of his best friends was in the greeting card business and he was going to be there. He told me that his friend was like the number one rep in the country for a card company that he couldn't remember the name of. I didn't think it was right for me to ask for a table at his event, so I didn't. I did ask for his friend's name, for I thought he might be able to help me with my cards. Perhaps he could rep my line! As we parted, he told me that his friend's name was Jordan and that he lived in Jerome, Arizona. He also told me to be careful, for he would try to recruit me. I thought that was a strange thing to say, for I was going to try to recruit him.

Well, we finally connected in June at a Starbucks in Phoenix. I came armed with my cards, which Jordan really liked.

He took me to his web site and we sent a card to Sherry. I thought it was cool how you could send a card from a computer. As I was sending the card, I was thinking about how convenient it was to send it. I picked out a card from a few thousand designs, didn't have to address it with my sloppy handwriting, didn't have to put it in an envelope, and I didn't have to find a stamp and mail it. I thought it was pretty cool.

I thought it could speed up the manual process that I was dealing with, that's for sure.

I remember asking how much it cost for a system like this and he said, "Less than $500.00."

Now, as you know, God works in mysterious ways, and that morning before arriving to meet Jordan, I got a little "God Wink." I got an invoice for $5800.00 worth of envelopes. I didn't need that many envelopes, but that's the amount that I had to order to get my pricing anywhere reasonable. I think God was trying to keep things in perspective for me financially.

But here's the God Wink that threw me over the top...I asked him who he worked for. I remember asking if he worked for Hallmark or American Greetings...I really didn't know the name. I thought he might work for a division. He said, "Oh, it's easy to remember; it's called Send Out Cards." When he said the name "Send Out Cards," you could have knocked me over with a feather! It wasn't a God Wink, it was more like a slap across my head. I was thinking, Oh, my God, oh, my God! I remember looking up to the sky with goose bumps all over my body, tears in my eyes, and saying to myself, *Is this what You meant when You sent me the message of send out the cards for my clients on that January 16th night?*

I was thinking, *this is really strange...this is something that I just can't ignore.*

He then went on to tell me about the history of the company and why it was started. He told me about how they were forming an advisory group called the "Eagle's Nest," and how they were looking for some leadership.

Here comes another God Wink...we had just built a home in Maine on the lake and the builder gave us a beautiful wood carved sign that simply says, "The Eagles Nest"!

I started thinking back to a personal development course that I had just taken when it asked me for accomplishments that I had growing up. The first one I listed was coming in first place selling, yup, you guessed it "greeting cards" in the fourth grade at Lincoln Elementary.

Remember the girl that I married? Did I tell you that we met during the summer of her junior year (going to be a senior)? Guess what she sent me every single day that entire year while I was away at college. You guessed it.

She sent me a card every day!

I guess you could say that it was "in the cards" that I'm in this crazy business.

JAMES PACKARD. *I was born in Augusta, Maine.*

Growing up I went to 11 different schools (five different high schools). My dad was in sales and every time he got promoted, we had to move and live in a new territory.

I was the kid with the lemonade stand. I was a newspaper carrier (actually was Carrier of the Year in the state of Florida).

I put myself though college…working days while going to school nights.

I went into sales after graduating from college and eventually started my own business with $500.00 and a dream. I built our copier business into one of the top 25 Sharp Distributorships in the U.S. (even though we were located in Maine).

I sold our business to Ikon Office Solutions before my 50th birthday.

One of the things that I'm most proud of was that the first five people that started with me were with me when we sold the business 25 years later.

I am also an inventor. I hold the patent to the Coffee Cover Lid. My partner and I hold patents to a few products that we've taken from concept to national sales. I've appeared on QVC over 20 times with some of our products.

I started my own greeting card company (my cards were in over 800 PetSmart stores).

I joined a network marketing company and was awarded runner-up and Distributor of the Year honors within my first three years. I've been among the top ten income earners for ten years.

The first two people I sponsored were my sons, who went on to win Runner-up and Distributor of the Year.

Some of the things that I am most proud of include: Jaycees Man of the Year for my city and then our state, Dale Carnegie Sales Course Instructor, and John Maxwell Certified Trainer.

I've been happily married for 45 years and have two wonderful sons and daughters-in-law (and one-and-a-half grandsons).

I love sales and marketing. I especially enjoy looking at other successful businesses' practices and adapting them to my business.

I'm a firm believer that what might be as common as dirt in one industry might have the effect of an atomic bomb in another.

To me success is the journey, not the destination.

James Packard
jim@jimpackard.com

13

Making A Difference – Making Memories
Kris Potts

December 31, 2004, was the day my life took an unexpected path. It was not exactly the direction I would have chosen, nor would have any of the others involved, but I know God has a plan for each of us and we don't always get a vote.

Never thought I would be a caregiver, especially not to my best friend of 35 years. In the early years of friendship we shared experiences and heartaches, frustrations with parents, boys and life, and wondered where ours would take us. In 1975 I was at a local university where I met my future husband. She met her future husband that year as well. I was married in the spring of 1977 and she married in the fall that same year. We spent several years just doing what young married couples do; spending time with family, celebrating holidays together, shopping and just enjoying life.

Fast-forward to Christmas 1984. We were both expecting our first child! We shared stories, compared notes, doctors, and shopped nursery themes. We discussed names, gender, expectations, dreams and fears for our unborn children. Then, that summer we buried her father. We were deeply saddened that he would not share in our children's births and that they would never have an opportunity to know him. I had our daughter and five short weeks later, her baby girl entered the world. They were as different as night and day. We continued with shared play

dates, birthdays and holidays. There were some rocky points in her marriage and she tried very hard to make it work, but eventually made the
difficult decision to divorce. To make things more difficult, the day before
Christmas Eve we discovered her mom had passed away in the night.
Her only sister was in California, undergoing treatment for breast cancer, and there was no other family around. She had a young child, no
second income, and plenty of bills. Within the next year she became
unemployed and promises of support from her ex were not fulfilled. Her
home was lost to foreclosure and severe depression followed.

I was there through it all. The tears, the anger, and the late night
phone calls of panic. I listened and helped out with bills as I could. We
still spent all holidays together, watched football games on weekends,
attended all the girls' recitals and concerts and celebrated their accomplishments, talking almost daily on the phone. Intertwined with our
happiness was pain. Her sister's cancer returned and she subsequently
lost her battle, my mother passed after a short illness, my sister-in-law
and niece passed away that same year, and I had major back surgery. We
laughed, we cried, we prayed, we carried on.

One summer afternoon in 2001 she called with a panic in her voice.
She had found a lump in her breast. That is when the real journey began.
The news was not good. We did the research, found a surgeon, an oncol-
ogist, and determined chemotherapy after surgery was her best option.
After losing her sister, her mind of course went to the worst outcomes.
I researched doctors, accompanied her to appointments, held her hand,
was her second set of ears, and tried to keep her upbeat. She was worried
about medical bills and the time off work. Surgery was scheduled; I slept
on a cot at the hospital. I listened to everything the doctors said, asked
questions, observed how to care for her once she went home, dispensed
meds, drained tubes, drove to post-op visits, drove her to infusions, sat
with her, took her home. I tried to find options to help with fatigue,
nausea, mouth ulcers, just to name a few, trying to help her be as comfortable as possible. I was the only family she had left and this was such
a horrible time to feel alone. She recovered, worked to make ends meet

and to dig out of the financial hole that accompanies a major illness. And life went on. We attended numerous games, recitals and performances of the girls as a family unit. The girls had grown up together since birth and special events in our lives were shared as a family.

Fast forward again to New Year's Eve 2004. My family and I had just returned from dinner and were settling in for a quiet evening at home. I got a phone call from her daughter. She was scared. "Something's wrong with Mom and I don't know what to do." It did not appear to be life-threatening, so we got in the car, drove over and took her to the hospital. Turned out they had been running errands all day and she "forgot" how to unlock the car. She almost rear-ended a car at a stop light because she "forgot" how to use the brakes. She also got "lost" driving home. Well, you can imagine the scene at the county hospital on New Year's Eve. It was a long wait to be seen. As we were going through triage and intake, I sensed concern from nurses as they reviewed her history and continued to ask questions. They took her back for an exam and we waited.

I remember feeling like I had been punched in the gut and sinking to the floor as the attending physician told me the cancer was back. It was in her brain, her lungs and liver. They were going to admit her and she would see the doctor in the morning to determine where to go from here. It was rather surreal, in the midst of the hugs and tears, in the middle of the ER, the nurses and doctors began counting down and wished each other a subdued Happy New Year. Through the chaos around us, her number one concern was for her daughter. I promised her that night her daughter would always have a home with us.

The early tests showed the cancer in the brain was inoperable. Considering the prognosis, she decided to not pursue the chemo and opted for quality of life. Radiation was chosen. The elephant in the room was money. The cancer in her brain affected areas that controlled motor function. She was no longer allowed to drive and she could not continue to work. Without employment, we were forced to look into alternative sources of income and subsidies. Being a single mother without outside financial support, her paycheck had been used for basics. She had a small health policy through her workplace, but it wouldn't even begin to cover the expenses she was facing. She had purchased a supplemental policy that proved to be a Godsend, but it was still not enough.

Our days were spent navigating the Internet, making phone calls, waiting on terminal hold, filling out applications for aid and assistance, explaining the circumstances over and over and over again. Most people were very helpful, sympathetic and compassionate, and went out of their way to help. Those individuals made a tremendous difference in the journey and restored our faith in humanity. We learned to acknowledge and be thankful for each and every one.

Anyone who has been affected by cancer knows the drill of doctor appointments. Before we could see this one, we needed clearance from that one, to file with the insurance we had to submit these forms; they only saw new patients on this day of the week. It was an ongoing juggling act with my days off, already scheduled appointments, and cash flow. I sat with her through every one of these appointments, just as I had a few years before. I held her hand when I could, got her to appointments and scheduled the next visits. We ran errands afterward as a way to get her outside; allowing her to enjoy the sunshine, the change of seasons, and to feel she was still part of the world. We were fortunate to get into a program that, along with her supplemental insurance, provided coverage for hundreds and hundreds of dollars in medications that were needed each day. We engaged with local charities and some governmental agencies, qualifying for a substantially reduced rent at the complex where she lived, where they waived policies for her benefit. Some of the organizations offered help with utilities and groceries, and we were grateful for even the smallest break or offer to help.

In addition, there was the practical side of things; an apartment full of furniture, belongings and mementos. It was an extremely emotional time, making piles of what she wanted to preserve. Several friends stepped up to the plate and offered assistance with this process. We'd pick a closet, show up with boxes and bags and disseminate her life, one room at a time. There were moments of hilarity, lots of reminiscing, lots of sharing and lots of tears. There were also moments for hard discussions; funeral arrangements, who would deliver a eulogy, flowers, music, where to be buried, legal issues. As things progressed her short term memory loss was the most noticeable and difficult to deal with. There were times when she would be so brave and so positive and at others, she was inconsolable. One moment that stands out was in her bathroom. Her hair was just about gone again and she asked me to shave off what was left. She sat on the toilet and cried. I carefully shaved her skull and cried with her.

Our hospice nurse was an angel in disguise. She taught me a lot of what was and would be needed, how to hook up oxygen tanks, how to change sheets with her in the bed, how to dispense meds when she could no longer swallow. One evening I got a call from the nurse and was told the end was near. I packed a bag and moved in for her final days. She slept a lot. The moments of lucidity became fewer and farther in between. Phone calls were made and a steady stream of visitors came to say goodbye. Her breathing became noisy and raspy. I slept with my hand on her arm because as long as I could feel the rise and fall of her breathing, I knew we still had her with us. The end came in the middle of the night. It seemed she was arguing with God. She would mutter "un uh" over and over. I pictured Him holding out His hand for her and her telling Him, "No, I'm not ready." His answer, of course, was, "Yes, My child, it's ok, it's time."

Sometimes the road we are purposed to travel does not make sense at the time, but we need to trust, observe lessons provided, and eventually the "why" will be revealed. Looking back I can see that my role was to be "the practical one," taking care of all the essential tasks while others took care of fun things to pass her days like making crafts, watching movies, painting nails, and buying pretty, frilly things to make her smile. I also look back and see God's hand in it all. I see her in her daughter and am reminded frequently of the many moments we shared together. I know she is safe and whole in the hands of God and we will always be connected. No matter how prepared we think we might be it still hurts deeply, but I am left with memories no one can steal and knowing that, in the end, my efforts made a difference. You never know the extent or impact your presence will have on another you have contact with. I am hopeful the fruit of the experience will be brought forth in the memories.

KRIS POTTS RDH, BS *was a clinical dental hygienist for 32 years, is an active member of the American Dental Hygienists' Association, accredited Provider with the American Academy of Dental Hygiene, and member of the American Academy for Oral Systemic Health. The Immediate Past President of the Texas Dental Hygienists Association, she currently represents the Spry Xylitol product line, offering information to a cross section of medical and dental offices in 10 states and presenting dental topics to consumer advocacy, support and special interest groups. She owns Oral Health Promotion Strategies, LLC, offering educational speaking, writing, and consulting services for dental professionals.*

Kris Potts
Oral Health Promotion Strategies LLC
5720 Windmere Ln.
Fort Worth, TX 76137
817-975-9446
KrisPottsRDH.com

14

A View From The Top Of The Box
Debbie Roman

My story is that of a transformational journey from unhappy, unhealthy, and unfulfilled to happy, athletic, and full of confidence and competence to inspire and motivate you to achieve your dreams. I changed my life completely beginning in 2013. I lost 117 pounds, started eating healthy and became a CrossFit athlete. Patience and tenacity have taught me a mantra of "Just Breathe." I know what rock bottom is and how to get out of that place, allowing my workouts and a healthy lifestyle to change me.

> *"…You are not who your past says you are. You are who you choose to be!…"*
>
> *Tyler Turner*

Transformation is so cliché, and we all think we know what it really means to transform, until that dark day when we have no other option. That day when the voices of doubt, of hatred, of ridicule cast such a dark shadow over your life and happiness that you just want to "flip the bird" to the world. You've become that mean girl, walking through life angry and just waiting for the other shoe to drop.

I am broken. I have been hurt. I have scars so deep they may never heal. But guess what, so do you. We all have our demons and skeletons. If you get really honest with yourself you will realize that without all that stuff you could never become the new, stronger version of you in the future. Debbie 2.0.14 came at a price, but that price has yielded the highest reward yet in my life. I have learned that the old skeletons and the bones they are made of make one dynamic scaffolding to rebuild the life I have always dreamed of.

Let's face it, unless you were the prom queen, star quarterback, rich kid, or top of class, you were probably like me, just another awkward kid in high school desperately wanting to fit in. My weight issues started in my 20s. I was tall and slender when I was younger. Obesity became a symptom of a much deeper problem, desperate to be recognized and a desire to please. In my 40s now, I was overweight, sick, depressed and very unhappy from a life of drinking, smoking, eating out, little to no sleep and a heaping pile of stress. I was on empty except for a successful career which I paid a heavy price for, and I saw that price each morning in the mirror. I was a wreck emotionally, spiritually and physically. I allowed a man to verbally assault me for years. I hit rock bottom and wallowed in it. But I ultimately pulled myself out one burpee, one jump, one WOD at a time.

I cannot erase the past, I have to embrace it. I am who I am because of it. I have learned that people will either love me or they won't. And those that would rather judge me, well, just remember, Karma is a force to be reckoned with.

What a difference a year makes. I am stronger physically and mentally. I am in better shape than I have been in a long time. Maybe ever. I've dropped 117 pounds. My confidence has skyrocketed and I have learned to push beyond my perceived limits. I now embrace my past, my age, and my position in life. I've learned to own it and to be proud of it, although some days are easier than others. After all, it is my experiences and years that brought me this far and I have yet to mess up completely. I also don't pretend to have achieved such a transformation alone. It took a community and a few Sweat Angels to get here. Along the way I have experienced some great adventures, faced some of the scariest moments, and learned lessons that have helped me silence my Food

Demons once and for all.

I could just list a bunch of lessons learned from working out with my personal trainer and incorporating CrossFit into my daily routine, but that would not paint the right picture. You see, there is a story here. One with a lot of pain, mentally and physically. Lifetime bonds formed with new friends, new perceptions of life, and an understanding of what it means to live, and, well, let's face it, a lot of laughs as I navigated my way around, lifting weights and jumping on boxes. So instead I am going to share the stories that ultimately taught me the toughest and most profound lessons of my life, and formed unbreakable bonds with my Sweat Angels. Ironically, many of these lessons hit me in the face...or shin...or thigh...at the box during the 5:00 am WOD.

We need to start with the basics, like what is CrossFit, or rather, what it is not. At its core, CrossFit is just a fitness program incorporating cardio, weight lifting, gymnastics, and core conditioning created by Gregg Glassman several decades ago. In CrossFit your goal is to optimize your fitness by performing high intensity, constantly varied functional movements, often against the clock and yourself in an accepting and encouraging environment. CrossFit workouts aim to prepare you for any physical challenge you may encounter in life, especially the unknown like the impending zombie apocalypse I keep hearing so much about. CrossFit is not for everybody; it's not even for the majority. In fact, it's the hardest thing I have ever done in my life. It takes nerves of steel and the determination of an ox. It's painful and often bloody, no one sings Kumbaya (although we all belt out a little Eminem every morning), and there are no bright lights, shiny machines, and mirrors. There is, however, a community like nothing I have ever seen. We all sweat, bleed, curse, cheer, cry, twerk a little, and FINISH together. We hold each other accountable and challenge each other when necessary. We have a strong common bond with CrossFit.

CrossFit is full of acronyms. Many of my non-CrossFit friends get lost in my "new" language, so to help keep everyone on the same page, here are the most common acronyms and their meanings. CrossFit gyms are often large warehouses, usually referred to as the "box." The daily workout is referred to as the WOD, Workout of the Day. We RX WODS, which means we completed the workout as written, with no scaling or modifications, with full range of motion. Experienced CrossFit athletes are referred to as Firebreathers. AMRAP, As Many Rounds (Reps) As Possible, means you put it all out there for the allotted time, trying to get the most rounds/reps possible and with any luck beating your best time or weight from previous similar WODS. Chippers are workouts with many reps and many movements (you chip away at it), typically completed in one single round for time. Toes-To-Bar (TTB) is a movement that is designed to test your abdominal and arm strength, as well as your grip strength, by getting both toes to touch the bar at the same time from a hanging position.

Just Keep Breathing Past Your Limits

The road out of the pain is paved with …burpees, freakin' burpees… and running and chippers!

Burpees…I hate burpees! Like really, really hate burpees, yet they have become one of the most significant movements to getting to where I am today. Simply put, a burpee is a squat, thrust to a plank position; do a push up, return to squat, then jump up. Simple, right? Maybe the first two, but then the burpee takes over your body for the remaining 25 —infinity (depending on just how sadistic the WOD is that morning). At about 15, your thighs will begin burning so bad you would swear there was acid on the floor. You take a step back, shake out your legs, breathe like it's your last breath, praying you misread the WOD and you are actually done. No such luck.

Then I hear Kyle Flowers, our head coach at CrossFit Annihilation, my friend, and one of my many Sweat Angels, "Keep moving guys, just keep moving." So I throw myself on the floor again, fighting off the nausea that now threatens to earn me a free t-shirt. Then, suddenly, I'm finished, laid out on the floor in a heap of sweat and yes, tears. As I try to catch my breath, I realize that I don't hate burpees, I love burpees! …or maybe my brain is just starved for oxygen and I am hallucinating. Either way, there is a lesson here.

You see, in order to get through high reps of burpees, or a long run, or one of Jeannice's chippers, you have to do two things: keep laser focus on one more rep, not the 50 you have to go, but one more perfect burpee until completion. Just keep moving. Just keep breathing. And second, throw all those self-proclaimed limitations out the door! Your thighs, your lungs, your shoulders will all conspire with that little voice inside your head to try to make you stop, quit, or fall into a typical pattern of remaining in your box where life is routine. You must keep fighting, fighting that burpee assault. Deep down in my soul I knew I was strong enough to fight for what I wanted. No matter how difficult the process, there was a way to become the person I was meant to be. That day I realized that this journey would be along a road paved with burpees... freakin' burpees.

Trust and Believe: Let Your Workout Change You

I heard it before: Working out is good for you and sitting around eating Cheetos, drinking Dr Pepper and watching TV is bad. I wanted a healthy lifestyle. I thought if I could get my body healthy then I could tackle the baggage I was carrying in my heart. I was counting on those exercise endorphins I had heard so much about pulling me out of my misery. You know, those brain chemicals that leave you feeling happier and more relaxed. It is far too easy to sit in the dark and hate yourself, to be so ashamed you can hardly move, but I knew I had to get up.

I had a membership to a well-known big box gym, but I had not been in there in years. Another pit of wasted money. That place made me feel so uncomfortable. Today's gym is not my scene. I am not impressed by a lot of fancy equipment with members who barely know the first thing about using it. Even worse is to watch as the opposite sexes ogle the skimpily clad bodies of the genetically blessed and pass judgment on everyone else. Most come to the gym only for social contacts and visual kicks, so any hope of finding real results was not in the cards.

Armed with this attitude, I started looking for an alternative. That is when I came across boutique training studios. There were two in Katy, so I chose the closest to my home, Premier Personal Training. I made my choice blindly, not using sound techniques for selection of a trainer. At that point in my life I was barely breathing; extensive research was out of the question. I would have to rely on minimal research and Divine intervention to get me to the right place. Fortunately, my faith held strong and God led me to the people that would help rescue me. This is where I met my trainer, friend, and, ultimately, my first Sweat Angel, Tyler Turner.

Tyler wanted me to maintain working out on my off days, but finding something that I would stick with was proving to be a challenge. I heard all the buzz about CrossFit, even seeing the games on TV once, which piqued my interest. What is CrossFit, anyway, and is it for me? Well, I wanted something different from the "gym" I was used to. I tried ellipticals, weight machines (gross), and Zumba classes, but either I found no benefit or my ADHD would have me bored in minutes and chasing another option. Then one night my neighbor, Georgia, introduced me to her best friend, Rhonda, while waiting on Santa to visit Heights Street last Christmas and, shall we say, my addiction was born. The best gift Santa ever brought me was the CrossFit Kool-Aid. I was soon a regular 5 am'er at CrossFit Annihilation.

Fast forward to box jumps, another functional movement that proves to be a metaphor for life—and I might add one of the scariest moves in CrossFit. Here is where I would face my fears or kill myself trying. Basically, from a standing position you jump with both feet on wooden boxes of varying heights. If you miss, you know it. You have not felt pain until you rack you shin off that box. I had been trying in class with little success, even earning my first CrossFit scar from a miss on my left shin that will be there for life. So when Tyler wanted me to jump, I was nothing short of nervous, although I did my best not to let it show. I have chosen to trust Tyler and he wouldn't have me do it if he thought I couldn't, right? But the truth is these terrify me. All I hear is, "Why are you doing this?" "You are going to hurt yourself!" "Girls of your size don't do jumps like that!" My size—where did that come from?

I am not the fat chick anymore! At my age and physical condition, was it not stupid to be doing what I was doing? Yet I followed direction and tried to steady myself, limiting eye contact, as that would give away my uncertainty and lack of confidence. He told me before he would not let me fall; could I believe that? Most people in my life have let me fall, to fend for myself, why not Tyler, too, even if it was just hitting the ground? I fell more than once growing up with nothing but the hard ground to stop the fall. Figure it out, they would say, toughen up, stop being so dramatic. Are you kidding me? So I did the only thing I knew...survive at all costs, bury the fear and fake it!

Seven jumps down and I was OK, even cutting up with Tyler, trying to maintain some level of confidence—God bless him, he puts up with me with such ease. Then I started the eighth jump...I felt it go wrong. The mind is a powerful thing, because in that split second all the pain and fear was right there. I saw the hurt of my past, felt the pain, and knew I was once again going to hit the ground, only this was real and it was going to hurt. I can take the physical pain, just wasn't sure if I could take the humiliation. My toe caught the bench and my body flew forward. Then something amazing happened—two arms caught me. They didn't strike me, they didn't push me away, they didn't blame me, they didn't let me fall; they caught me. It was Tyler. He always told me he would not let me fall. Not sure I was able to fully believe him until that night.

All I wanted to do was finish my last two jumps; I was not going to get emotional, not there. It was not the place. So I brushed it off with my usual flippant attitude and told him I was fine. Maybe God had hold of that foot, maybe I am just a big klutz, but for the first time in my life someone I trusted did not let me down, he was true to his word. All the weight I have lost, all the strength I have gained means nothing...I trusted and was not disappointed.

This carried over to CrossFit. Trust was now a central part of my life again, not only in others but also in me. But as the weeks passed, slowly I faced my deepest fears and realized that no one laughed at me, only with me. More important, I realized that what I needed most were support and encouragement. CrossFit is built on a support system. I have never had anyone believe in me personally or stand behind me the way that Tyler, Kyle, and the 5 am'ers, the third piece of the Sweat Angel puzzle, have. They believe I can do it when I have a hard time believing in myself. I work harder to finish every workout faster because I have my 5:00 am crew screaming my name and cheering me toward the finish line.

Commitment and Dedication: Wine is Paleo, Right?

Everything I had been through taught me one thing: food was my crutch. I had used it for years as my "drug of choice." Who needed pot, pills, or other substances when I could have donuts, gravy, and pizza! Hence, my Food Demons controlled me. Anytime I needed a boost, I went for sugar and carbs and lots of them. If I was sad, that called for brownies and ice cream; if I was happy, well that meant Starbucks and brownies; depressed meant as much Mexican food as I could stand; stress was particularly nasty, as it would mean mounds of sugar in the form of candy, donuts, and yes, more brownies; and lonely would always find me belly up to the table at any number of home-cooking restaurants, gorging on anything covered in old-fashioned cream gravy.

First thing I had to do was accept that food was no longer going to be my security blanket, it was fuel for the body I wanted. Just like I wouldn't put cheap gas in a high-performance car, I should not put poor quality food into my body. This meant really understanding what our bodies were designed to eat. Easier said than done! After a lot of research on clean eating, I decided to embrace the Paleo diet, beginning with the Whole 30. Basically, I was going to detox my body from grains, bread, sugar, dairy, and processed carbohydrates for 30 days, then level out with embracing the Paleo lifestyle.

I decided to remain strict until I reached my weight loss goals; only then would I begin to go 90/10. I just couldn't go all in; I love my wine, even completing my level one sommelier certification. I just did not see myself giving up a glass of wine in moderation, so that was my Paleo modification, the occasional adult beverage. There were still plenty of hard realities to go around...foods I loved were now off limits, that was going to be a tough one. My old lifestyle included Mexican food three or four times a week, bread with every meal, gallons of milk a week, and dessert every night. In the four years prior since my divorce I am not sure that I even turned on the stove. Did it still work? Could I learn to cook? I had to accept that what I was used to simply did not fit the new Debbie 2.0.14.

I had a good grasp of what was a clean food and what wasn't, so one Sunday morning I decided to rid the house of all the NO foods. I knew baby-steps was not my style, so I drug in the trash can and began to say goodbye to boxes of brownie mix, hamburger helper, canned everything, cookies, chips, you name it. I tried to sort out what I could take to the food bank. After all, in my head I was adding up the dollars going into that trash can. As I reached the bottom of the pantry there they were, a brand new 12 pack of Dr Pepper. I actually had a physical reaction to the thought of tossing them. My body got hot and I was trembling. *This must be what it is like to come off meth,* I thought to myself. I knew there was absolutely no nutritional value in sodas. No vitamins. No minerals. High concentration of sugar. But none of that mattered. I had been drinking Dr Pepper for as long as I could remember; it was part of my brand. As hard as it is to admit, I opened the 12-pack and pulled one can out and placed it in the fridge, mentally putting a sign on it that read, "In case of emergency, drink this." I guess I am a true work in process, because that can is still in my fridge, right where I placed it on trash day.

I made it through trash day. My pantry was bare. Now I needed to re-stock. I remembered a few things Tyler and Kyle had said as I embarked on my first real trip to Whole Foods.

Number one rule was to shop the perimeter of the store buying fresh fruit, vegetables, meats and seafood. I could buy frozen fruits and veg-etables to make meals easier during the work week. I was only to go down the aisles for select things like nuts, olives, coffee, etc. I learned the center of the store is generally one big, processed, nutritionally worth-less carb-fest. But, man, was it tempting at first! Over time, I adjusted quite well and found the Paleo lifestyle to fit me perfectly. I look back now and can't believe I ever ate so much sugar and processed foods. My body now rejects it, in unique and creative ways I might add!

I am a Firebreather!

Life is not all about the pain or hurt, it really is about what you do with that pain and hurt. Ultimately, I have channeled mine into my workouts. I bring it all into the box each morning and to my workouts in the evening, the good, the bad, the ugly, the scars, and the bruises; but I leave it there, on the barbell, in the bucket of chalk, or sweat pools on the floor. I have embraced the idea that callouses are sexy, bruises on shoulders are cool, everyone can twerk—especially Matt—everything is better with the right soundtrack, and for God's sake you cannot use enough chalk when doing toes-to-bar!

Some say CrossFit is a cult and, well, let's face it, some of the behavior fits nicely into the definition of a cult, like referring to ourselves as Firebreathers, and any true CrossFitter knows that Paleo is the only way to eat. Lululemon and Nano are the unofficial uniforms and our mascot is a puking clown—need I say more? If this is a cult, then I proudly stand on top of that box after RX'ing a butt-kicking WOD, in my Nano 4.0s, holding my post-workout protein shake, sporting a new burnout tank inscribed with *I Can Deadlift You*, screaming TIME! ◼

DEBBIE ROMAN *has always been a high achiever, starting with education, achieving her masters from University of Houston along with an impressive array of credentials and certifications. She's at the top of her profession as a highly-accomplished Organizational Effectiveness Manager with a track record of managing complex organizational change management and performance improvement projects.*

She is a longtime volunteer in the community with an award from the mayor for her contributions. But Debbie's secret was a personal life mired in unhappiness and unhealthy living. Then she changed her life completely. She lost 115 pounds, started eating healthy and became a CrossFit athlete at CrossFit Annihilation. Debbie is a tremendously inspiring motivational speaker and life coach who knows what rock bottom is and how to get out of that place. She has become more than just a career; she's now a fully rounded person who is better at everything because of it. Debbie has learned how to love life and herself, and she has enthusiasm and wisdom to share with her audiences and clients as she inspires them to find the way up out of whatever place they find themselves and embrace the world that is waiting for them.

Debbie Roman
Houston, Texas
debbieroman@consolidated.net
www.debbieroman.com
713-805-6193

15

Horse Power: My Key To Freedom

Kathy Taylor

As a child, how many times did you hear, "Sticks and stones may break my bones, but words will never hurt me"?

Maybe you even said the phrase yourself. I know I did, and it was precisely because the words *did* hurt.

I would venture to say that emotional wounds from words cause more damage than most childhood physical wounds. While physical wounds can leave a scar on the outside, wounds from words may never heal. Because these scars are internal, no one but us knows they're there. With time it gets easier to ignore them and pretend they've gone away. But the hurt remains—and it shapes who we are from the inside out.

This is the story of how hurtful words imprisoned me—and how I broke through, became whole, and now use that experience of overcoming to empower others to break free from their own limitations. It's a story I hope will inspire you to stage your own jailbreak from the bondage that holds you back.

Horse Crazy

There is no doubt about it: I was born with the horse-crazy gene. Horses are part of my DNA.

As a child, I trotted and cantered everywhere I went, whether I had four strong legs to carry me or just my own to take me where I was going. Regardless, I could whinny with the best of them. I collected Breyer Horse models, read every horse story I could get my hands on—from every *Misty of Chincoteague* book there was to all the adventures of *The Black Stallion* and, of course, *Black Beauty*. On the playground, my grade school friends and I pranced and reared, snorted and galloped as if we lived on the open prairie with the wildest of herds.

In other words, I LOVED horses. I still do. (Don't tell anyone, but I still occasionally canter around when no one is looking.)

As I became a teenager, my love of horses continued to grow. My fellow horse-pretending playmates became fewer and further between as they found other things that interested them more. Each Christmas, a horse was at the top of my wish list, even though I knew it would never happen. Maybe you knew a little girl like this. *Maybe you were one.*

Growing up so seriously bitten by the horse bug was lonely. No one among my family or friends understood the depth of my love for these creatures. Horses were powerful and strong, yet could be very gentle and quiet. I knew beyond a doubt that horses were good for me, and that I was good for them.

This connection was strengthened when, after my favorite pony, Pinstripe, fell gravely ill, my trainer assigned me alone to care for her and bring her back to the spunky pony she once was. My trainer's belief that I could handle such a big responsibility caused my confidence to soar. It made me feel like I had something to contribute. It was a way for me to give back to the horse that gave me such joy.

Unexpected "Neigh-sayers"

In the eighth grade, one of my school friends started taking riding lessons at "my barn." Finally, someone else to share my passion! We knew the same horses, shared similar experiences. When I talked about Shenanigan or Sandy and the quirks of their personalities, she understood completely.

At school, our "spot" was under a massive oak tree where we ate lunch every day with a big group of girls. One day, as I walked toward my friends with my cafeteria tray, a spray of hurtful words stopped me in my tracks.

"*Oh, great.* Here comes Kathy. *Now* all we're going to hear about is those *stupid* horses."

I fought back the tears, feeling like I'd been punched in the gut. Nevertheless, I smiled and pretended everything was fine. The truth was that I felt wounded at my core. Because so much of my identity—*of who I was*—was wrapped up in horses, I felt completely rejected.

A Promise Made of Pain

Right then and there, I made a promise to myself that I would never bring up the subject of horses again. Having overheard those hurtful words, I was convinced that nobody cared about what mattered to me. Desperate for people to like and accept me, I knew if I wanted to fit in, I had to keep quiet about "the horse thing."

Little did I know how much that vow would shape the rest of my life.

For the next few decades (call me a slow learner), I was very careful *not* to talk about my passion—even with other fellow horse lovers. Despite my silence, however, horses were still the biggest part of my life. I spent hours riding and hanging out at the barn with them. On Saturdays, my dad dropped me off at 8:00 am on his way to work and picked me up at 6:00 pm on his way home. The barn was always my favorite place to be. The smell of leather and sweat was better than the finest perfume. During summers in college, I worked at a guest ranch in Colorado. Talk about a dream job! I got *paid* to ride a horse all day, every day, in the majestic Rocky Mountains!

Love, Expanded

Most girls lose their interest in horses when boys and dating become part of the picture. Not me, however.

I admit that by the time I met my husband, Tim, I was getting tired of hiding my passion. Horses were a part of me and if someone was going to truly love me *for me*, accepting horses was part of the package.

My first date with Tim ended up being a last-minute thing. I had already planned to spend the day with my horse, Reno. I invited Tim to come along as a test of his willingness to accept my intense "horsiness." Reno needed new hay, his stall mucked out, and new shavings added. Romantic, huh? Fortunately, Tim took it all in stride (pun intended). It didn't hurt that Reno liked Tim, too. Although I've never been able to convert Tim to a horse lover, to this day he fully accepts and supports my horse craziness.

Something About Motherhood

Scars from my 8th grade rejection showed up again when I became a mother. Still wanting to fit in—even if it cost me my joy—I recognized how much I was willing to keep quiet and not make waves so other people would like me.

I knew this was not a good thing. "People pleasing" was certainly not something with which I wanted to infect my children. Raising confident children who would bounce back when the boat got rocked was my dream.

My son, Ben, has never lacked in the confidence department. He's always been equally comfortable with adults and children. One day when he was about five, he told me about a situation with friends at school and how he was going to handle it the next day. I was afraid his solution wouldn't go over well with the other kids, and I suggested that he not say what he had planned.

"Why not?" was his pointed question.

Knowing how detrimental my desire to be liked above all else had been to me, I had already determined that I was not going to plant "that" seed in the mind of my child. Sending the message that it was more important to keep quiet so people will like you than it is to be your true self was not an option. Still, my fear caused me to waver.

In my mind, the argument with myself went something like this:

You have to tell him not to say that. They won't like him if he does.

No! Kathy, don't say it. Don't infect him.

But he's only five years old. He doesn't know any better. You have to protect him.

Don't say it, Kathy. It's evil. You don't want to poison him with the people-pleasing disease.

And the words came out, "Because they won't like you."

Aaagghh! WHY did I say that? I didn't want to say that!

In that moment I felt like a complete failure as a mother. I had stifled the voice of my child.

Then Ben responded. "So what?"

In my mind I said, *"Hallelujah! I didn't infect him after all! He rejected it. He's confident enough in himself that he doesn't seek the approval of others."*

It was true. The five-year-old provided the shining example of standing up for your values.

Walking in Faith

Even in my elation that Ben didn't succumb to the identity-stealing trap of "other people's approval," I still struggled with meeting others' expectations. I was still willing to hide part of myself in order to be accepted.

In my late 30s my faith really took a turn back to God. However, just as I avoided talking about horses so people would like me, I was also not willing to talk about God because I wanted people to like me. Religion can be very divisive and, as you already know, I am not a fan of conflict. To me, it was still far more comfortable to say nothing and let others fill in the blanks than to open my mouth and take a stand.

In my effort not to offend anyone, I simply left God out of any conversation unless someone else mentioned Him first. Now I was not only stifling the passion for horses that God gave me, I was also stifling the power of God in my life.

By the time we moved to Texas in 2007, I was pretty sure the whole 8th grade incident was far behind me; I hadn't thought about it in years. However, when I followed my passion and my faith and started a business that helps people become better leaders at work, at home, or at school by learning from the wisdom of horses, middle school voices started chattering again.

Not only did I have to share my passion for horses with non-horse people, I had to explain to them that their lives could be different as a result of interacting with them. (And, by the way, you won't be riding them either.) Beyond not "liking" me, people were going to think I was crazy!

Things were different now; I had faith on my side. When I was in the arena with a client, I knew without a doubt that I was doing what God meant for me to do. I was simply calling on my God-given passion and appreciation for how beautifully and humbly animals—especially horses—will serve and love us if we are open to the opportunity. Combining my deep-seated passion for horses and my natural desire to help people set themselves free from the obstacles in their lives made my light shine as never before.

Still unsure of my true value, the questions I asked myself were these: Was I willing to risk rejection and let this light shine for *all* the world to see? Would this leap of faith empower me to share the other parts of me out loud? Did I really have the courage to stop hiding, speak up, and really be me?

As I've continued the journey, I've surprised myself with my courage to persist. While the challenges I've conquered may appear small to some, they represented mountains to me as I struggled with the underlying belief that I just wasn't worth listening to. Somehow, I found the determination to keep going and claim each victory, step by step.

Willing to Be Unpopular

One of the symptoms of "people pleasing-itis" is that you have a hard time setting boundaries—especially with "important people." It's that inner voice reminding you that "they won't like you if you tell them what to do."

The first time I was able to meet this challenge with my newfound confidence occurred when several executives from a large corporation came to observe a team development workshop I was delivering. By the time the "important people" arrived, the session was well underway. One particular executive, keenly interested in all that was happening, was asking some great questions.

With a certainty that surprised me, I paused the session and calmly and confidently explained to this "important person" that my first commitment belonged to the client currently in the arena, but I would be able to talk with him—and answer all his great questions—*after* the session. Of course, he understood completely and was not upset in the least. This turned out to be a defining moment for me. It was the first time I can remember consciously choosing to set a boundary and not worry about offending someone who, frankly, intimidated me.

It's so good to finally be at a point where (most of the time, at least) I am able to stand up with abundant confidence for what I know is the best and right thing.

Unlocking Freedom

Through this journey I've learned that the key to freedom is hearing God. His words never hurt and always heal. Since He created my passion for horses, He also knows that communicating through them is the best way to get my attention. When I start listening to the negative banter bouncing around in my own head, I ask God to remind me who I am.

How ironic that the love for horses that once kept me quiet and playing small is now a source of strength and inspiration to me and to others through my work. With their grace, beauty, power, strength and spirit, horses are the embodiment of freedom.

Now that I've shared my passion with you, it's time to turn the focus to you!

Your passion helps you to identify *your* purpose. It helps you define who you are—and how you are uniquely different from every other person ever created. You were created for a very specific purpose that you alone can fulfill. If you aren't willing to break through the words or emotions that imprison you to create the masterpiece of your life, we *all* miss out.

Imagine Van Gogh's *Starry Night* painted without yellow! Something would most definitely be missing. Just like that painting, without *your* unique contribution, our world is a little less colorful.

I urge you to spend some time and thought discovering and reconnecting with who you are at your core. Don't allow words to hold you hostage for decades like I did! Discover your own beauty, grace, speed and the power you need to break free from what holds *you* back.

A passion for horses is what God gave me as a way to transform not only my life but the lives of my clients. If the *real* you is just *waiting* for a jailbreak, I dare *you* to regain your voice, reclaim your courage, and rediscover your own uniqueness to make the difference you were meant to make. ■

KATHY TAYLOR *is a leadership coach, engaging speaker, and CEO of HerdWise, an interactive leadership development company.*

Through her unique ability to see and understand your story, Kathy pulls back the curtain on exactly why you play small. She pinpoints the core lies you believe so that you experience the truth about the impact you were created to have.

Kathy's coaching clients report "core level changes about their beliefs" that really stick. In her transformational workshops and retreats, Kathy opens your eyes to the power behind passion and purpose. New ways of seeing, thinking and living are established by interacting with horses in structured non-riding activities.

Certified by EAGALA as an Equine Specialist, Kathy is a lifelong learner and has also been trained in Equine Guided Education and Results Coaching.

Kathy was awarded the Innovator Spirit Award by the National Association of Women Business Owners. Don't miss her TEDx Talk, Harness the Power of the Whisper, at www.tedxtalks.ted.com/.

If you would like to improve your relationships, communication or leadership, please contact Kathy Taylor.

Kathy Taylor
Leadership & Confidence Coach, Speaker, Author
Kathy@HerdWise.net
www. HerdWise.net

154

16

Dreams To Reality
Janna Valencia

Everyone has a dream, a desire to do something meaningful in life, to make a difference. What we don't know is how to take that dream and turn it into reality to make the difference in our life and our world. I want you to know that we all make a difference in life but many of us don't know how to realize it.

I was born in a small East Texas town. I was raised by loving parents, but when I was 13 they divorced. That was a difficult time for my parents and the four children. We lived with our mom, who worked two or three different jobs to make sure that we did not lack anything.

Although I did not understand many of the things she did or why she did them, I knew she never gave up and she always seemed to be so positive about everything. At least, that is the way I saw it then. Today, it is very clear that what she did was because she had a dream and she was going to make that dream a reality. She wanted to make a difference in her life, the lives of her children, and of those that were in her sphere of influence. Each day that passed she instilled in us the qualities of honesty, integrity, character, loyalty, and the value of hard work.

At the age of 17, armed with passion and desire, I left my small East Texas home to discover a world unknown to me. I was unprepared for what lay ahead of me. I received all of the motivation to get out there and make a difference in the world but I didn't pay attention to the "rest of the story," which was that I needed to have clear direction of my destination and why.

I fell in love with a boy from high school. What I thought was going to be a "happily ever after" situation started a sequence of events that would change my life and take me into many situations that were very painful. Thanks to the fortitude that my mom was able to instill in me, and the saving grace of Jesus Christ, I was able to overcome drug addiction, mental and physical abuse, and the pain of a failed marriage.

I entered into a career in retail sales. There, I quickly rose to the top and became a manager. I spent 25 years in this career, and it was there that I learned why my mom forced us to listen to some guy we didn't know talking about something that bored us to tears. We would have rather been listening to our rock n' roll music. I began to read and listen to some of the same authors and speakers that she made us listen to. By the way, I was enjoying it. The messages started to make sense to me and I began to apply them to my life. I began to think about what the rest of my life would look like and how to make it happen.

In 2005, I met a man who was working for the same company as I. He also worked another job, at night, cleaning businesses. We became friends and later an opportunity arose for him to invest in that cleaning company. He asked if I would help him and invest in this business with him. I knew nothing about the commercial cleaning business but I had faith in him and in myself. Together, we invested in this business. We quickly realized that the other partner had very different ideas about how the income should be used, so we decided to dissolve that partnership and started our own cleaning company.

I continued to work at my full-time job and marketed the business on my days off. In less than a year, I had to make a decision to stop marketing our company or leave my job. My job was very secure, but I knew that if I devoted my time to the business it would grow quickly and I could replace my income. I made the decision to quit my job. I was scared and nervous. What if it didn't work? At the same time, I was excited because I knew that it could be something big.

Each year the company doubled its gross revenue, reaching $1 million in sales at the end of the third year. There were many struggles and hard lessons learned. The fourth year we opened another branch in a different metropolitan city, and at the end of the fifth year we reached $1.5 million in gross revenue.

That year we sold the business, allowing us to pay off all of our debt, and allowing me to move back to East Texas to be closer to family. It has also allowed me the time to organize and plan the newest venture of my life, my dream become reality.

In 2014 I formed a new company, MVP Products. This company has evolved from a simple product into a company that is helping people like you channel their dreams and turn them into reality.

In September 2014, MVP was only three months old, and although I had a plan, there was an element missing. By chance or Divine intervention, I watched a webcast hosted by the proud son of Zig Ziglar, Tom Ziglar. He was talking about keeping his father's legacy alive by teaching others to deliver his father's message through a certification program they were conducting. This was the missing element. I had the experience, success, and the desire to teach others, but with the Ziglar Legacy Certification I would have the educated ability to deliver it using the invaluable information taught by the legendary Zig Ziglar.

For those of you who do not know who Zig Ziglar was, I will give you a summary of his life and accomplishments.

Zig was born in 1926, in a small town in "LA," lower Alabama. He was the 10th of 12 children. His father died when he was five years old and he was raised by his God-fearing mother who instilled the values that would bring him through his life. In 1947 he dropped out of college and began selling full-time for a cookware company. After two years of struggling, his boss, P.C. Merrell, told him how he was wasting his talent and then told him how he had the potential to be the best. This conversation changed his life. By 1951 he became the #1 salesperson of 3000.

In 1970, he decided to devote all of his time to speaking and in 1974 he wrote his first book, *See You at the Top*. From 1974 to 2012 he authored over 31 books, many of which have been translated and distributed in many other countries. Most of his books have also been recorded on audio and video.

Zig Ziglar died in 2012, two days after his 66th wedding anniversary with the love of his life, Jean.

He is estimated to have impacted over 250 million lives with his inspirational message of hope.

I have integrated all of this together and now have a plan that is complete and will help you find the inspiration and knowledge to take your dream and make it a reality.

I wrote this chapter in hope that it will help you see that it doesn't matter who you are, where you came from, or what you have been through, you CAN achieve your dreams. ■

JANNA VALENCIA, *is a 30-year veteran of business growth and management. She specializes in helping people identify their dreams and make them reality.*

She was born in a small East Texas town learning the values of hard work at a young age.

Having aspirations to become a difference maker in the world, she began her ascent to entrepreneurism through the corporate world of retail. She started her career in sales, learning essential skills of business success, and moved into management, increasing her skills to include marketing, operations, administration and leadership.

She has built successful businesses, achieving her dreams and realized that the experience she gained is applicable in everyone's life, personally and professionally. She developed a desire to share what she has learned with others, helping them learn that they can achieve everything in life they want.

She now uses her years of experience in the "hard knocks" of life, corporate training, business ownership, and her Ziglar Legacy Certification to inspire and train others to make their dreams a reality.

"Achieving your life's dreams is nothing more than a decision to make it happen, a determined reason why you want it, a good plan, and a lot of fortitude."

Janna Valencia

You may contact Janna through email at:
janna@MyMVPproducts.com.

Visit her website at:
MyMVPproducts.com

17

The Excellence Effect

J. Justin Young

If success is your desired destination, then excellence is the vehicle that will take you there.

J. Justin Young

Excellence is defined as the quality of being outstanding or extremely good. Its Latin root, excellere, means "to surpass." I believe that deep within all of us lies the desire for excellence, the desire to be an outstanding individual who is extremely good at what he or she does—an individual of high moral character, of good reputation, a shining example to our family and community. We do not just want to be good; we want to be better than good, surpassing every limitation. Excellence is not mystical; there is no magic formula. Excellence is achieved by what we do or do not do on a daily basis. Excellence is a decision. Aristotle said it like this: "We are what we repeatedly do. Therefore, excellence is not an act but a habit."

I believe that excellence honors God and inspires people. At the moment that you begin to do the very best with what you've been given, at that moment excellence will begin to affect every area of your life, bringing a profound effect on the quality of your life. The great American football coach, Vince Lombardi, said, "The quality of a person's life is in direct proportion to his or her commitment to excellence, regardless of his or her field of endeavor."As people are inspired by your example and the spirit of excellence that you embody, a power is released that brings key relationships into place. Excellence brings in multiplication where previously only simple addition had existed. What I am describing will help you be, do, and have more in life. What I am describing is called "The Excellence Effect."

The desire to excel in our field of endeavor, our relationships, our finances, and every aspect of life is ingrained deep within our DNA. The truth is that no child grows up wanting to live a life of mediocrity or lack. As children we wake up with excitement, the world holds opportunity, and we can't wait to grow up and BE something! How often do you hear children telling everyone what they want to be when they grow up? I have three children at home, and I can tell you that they are sincerely optimistic; they're excited about what the future holds. Zig Ziglar said it like this:"Man was designed for accomplishment, engineered for success, and endowed with the seeds of greatness."

So if we all are born with the seeds of greatness inside us, if it is in our DNA as human beings to live a life of accomplishment and success, what happens to so many people? Why do they seem to be just surviving, simply dragging their way through life? Let me tell you from experience that life has a way of beating you down if you let it. Somewhere between school ending and adulthood beginning many people begin to become disengaged and disillusioned. Reality begins to hit and what our parents always referred to as"the real world"begins to become real on a whole new level.

We find that things don't just fall in our lap, but that we are going to have to begin to put in effort like never before, work extremely hard, and sometimes even fight when necessary. Oftentimes, after years of working, trying, fighting for our dreams, goals, and visions, we become weary. Complacency sets in, and we just give up. We keep working, we do what we need to do to survive, but we surrender to a mundane existence. We settle for a life of mediocrity and believe the lie that all we will ever be is average. Can I tell you that you were not created to merely survive, you were created to thrive! You were created to live a life of excellence!

Excellence vs. Perfection

I've found that many times people shut down and turn off their receptors the moment they hear the word "excellence," especially when it's spoken in terms of a core value to be put into practice for their daily life. It's almost as if you just slid a giant mountain in front of them and yelled, "Now climb!" The very thought of tackling that mountain is so daunting that they throw their hands up and say, "What's the use?" They simply give up. The challenge seems too big, the mission too consuming. I sincerely believe, after a decade of working with people, that it's not that most people are lazy or intentionally belligerent when it comes to living in excellence, it's that they think excellence is something else altogether! It's a case of mistaken identity.

Excellence has an impostor—it's called "perfection." The greatest enemy of excellence will always be perceived perfection. Let me say clearly that perfection has nothing to do with excellence. And let me parenthetically inject that neither does success. Let's call perfection what it is—an illusion! It's not real, it doesn't exist. Perfection is the hallucination of a dangling carrot leading individuals down a twisted, tiring rabbit trail with no destination in sight. It will rob you of peace, joy, and love, leaving you broke, busted, and disgusted in the end. Chasing perfection will leave you with a life of regret. Pursuit of what we perceive to be perfection leaves a wake of loss in our life—loss of time, relationships, finances, and authentic opportunities.

So I get it. Just talking about it is exhausting. But don't give up on excellence just because of what someone told you it would require. In a world where something better is always marketed to us in a way to make us dissatisfied with what we currently have or the way we may look, it's sometimes hard to keep our focus. Don't drink the Kool-Aid. The pursuit of perfection will kill your God-given passion. The practice of excellence fuels those God-given passions and empowers your dreams, your visions, and your goals.

Understanding the Excellence Effect

To fully understand the Excellence Effect we must first have a complete understanding of the terms associated with this concept. One of the most commonly mistaken grammatical errors is the usage of "Affect versus Effect." I'll be the first to admit that I have struggled with this one myself from time to time. Affect, with an "a," means "to influence." An example of usage would be: "The cold weather has affected my body temperature." Affect is most commonly used as a verb. Effect, with an "e," is usually a noun with many subtle meanings; however, at their core you will always find that effect is "a result." An example of usage here would be: "The cold temperatures had no effect on me," or "The sound effects were awesome." Lastly, we use the term "infect." When we think of this term we automatically think about sickness or disease. We immediately associate it with some aspect of the human body or medical field, although at its root infect simply means "to invade, penetrate, and permeate." Affect, Effect and Infect are the key components in a quote I use that represents the core process by which the Excellence Effect takes place in my life and yours.

> *The Affect of Excellence will always produce the Effect of Excellence and the effect of excellence will Infect every aspect of your life.*
>
> J. Justin Young

Excellence really is contagious! It catches on and has a dramatically positive effect on life. When my wife and I had our first child it brought so much in my life full circle. I saw things in a much greater depth than I had previously. I now saw the world through the eyes of a father! I instantly realized that there were so many layers to life that I had not previously known. Granted, they had been there all along, but I was unaware. Like many, I thought I knew how I would feel as a father. I would listen to parents talk so descriptively about how different they instantly felt and how the world changed. I knew, obviously, that much responsibility would come, and that life would change as it pertained to schedules, demands, and amounts of sleep, but I never realized the weightiness of what they were explaining. I will never forget the moment that our daughter was delivered and I heard her first cry. I felt like Neo in the sci-fi action movie The Matrix. I felt as if I had just been connected to a whole new world, a world much more alive, more vibrant, and with a now greater purpose than I had previously known.

Now, several years later, I have come to realize the beautiful effect that a newborn child has. The child affects not just the parents, but everyone the child touches—grandparents, aunts, uncles, cousins, family friends, church congregations. Everything changes; there's no going back! The covenant of love between my wife and me had affected us. The affect made possible for a moment of conception. That conception took us through a process that gave us another effect as our precious daughter was born, and the effect of that birth instantly and supernaturally infected our entire family and many friends with a new depth and quality of life and love that we had not formerly known.

Excellence in the same way will affect, effect, and infect every area of your life if you are committed to it. You must first make a covenant with yourself to practice excellence. It must become a daily habit that you pick up and put on as you would your tie or your shoes. You don't have to pursue it. You need not chase after it. You have it already. You must simply practice it. Excellence is developed by persistent consistency. Doing the small things daily will give you big results over time. If you are consistently faithful with the small things, eventually you will be given much.

You were placed on this earth with everything you need. You were equipped before the foundation of the world. It may come as a surprise to you, but every tool you need is already on board. Excellence is resident in you.

Get a Vision
To begin to operate in Excellence you must first get a vision for what excellence in your life will look like. It is paramount that you understand that vision will always empower your mission. We have a great ability, the ability to be able to see something before it ever physically manifests.

I call this faith.

Faith is the substance of things hoped for and evidence of things not yet seen. Faith is the power that enables visionary leaders like you and me to be able to look out and see what can be in areas that may seem barren to the natural eye. It is going to take faith to carry out your vision. There will be difficult times as you move forward, times of hardship, times of doubt. It will not be easy but it will be worth your effort.

I love how novelist E.L. Doctorow describes having vision in a difficult time—what I often refer to as a "night season.""It's like driving a car at night. You never see farther than your headlights, but you can make the whole trip that way." Sometimes, life clouds our vision and we cannot see clearly or see as far perhaps as we previously could, but as Zig Ziglar said, "When you begin moving towards your goals, just travel as far as you can see, and once you get there you'll be able to see even further."

I spell the word faith, R-I-S-K. Faith will always require an element of risk. It is imperative that you buy into your vision, that you yourself are all in, 100 percent sold, so that as you take a risk and step out in faith towards excellence, difficulty and negativity will not be able to detour you. The only failure in life is the person who fails to get up after falling. A vision is much more than seeing: It is believing; it is an experience. The great thing about a person with an experience is that they are never at the mercy of a person with an opinion.

One of my favorite books is *Leadership Excellence*, written by Pat Williams. Among the many stories about great leaders highlighted in this book, a particular story about Walt Disney resonates with me and gives what I believe is a stellar example of moving in faith toward your vision.

In the 1950s Walt Disney began to meet with teams of architects, engineers, and contractors as preparations were being made to begin construction on Disneyland. It was a huge undertaking and much planning would be required before beginning construction of the new theme park. As the initial plans were laid out, the team of professionals assembled all agreed that it would be wise to begin with the outer areas of the park and work their way inward. This would enable them to use roads, water, and all existing infrastructure as they worked their way in to the center of the park.

The center of the park is where the princess's castle was going to be, and working from the outside inward would save a tremendous amount of time and financial resources. While this made sense from the standpoint of conventional wisdom, Walt did not agree. He proceeded to explain to his team that they would approach the construction in reverse, building the princess's castle first and then working their way outward. You see, Walt Disney wanted that castle to tower over the park grounds so that every day as workers arrived they would see the excellence of what they were building. He wanted them to be able to catch his vision and be inspired to carry out the rest of the park with the same excellence. While this made no sense to some, it made perfect sense to Walt Disney, because he was the visionary.

Walt saw Disneyland long before anyone else. That castle that was once just a dream and a vision is now one of the most recognizable brands in the world—an international symbol of excellence, of what is now a multibillion-dollar company that has brought joy and changed the lives of countless children all over the world.

Your vision, or how you approach your vision, may not always make sense to everyone. Walt Disney's certainly didn't. But trust your heart. You may have to contradict popular opinion or what conventional wisdom may tell you, but don't allow contrary opinions, negativity, or current lack to keep you from moving forward. Keep trusted advisors close and guard your vision from adversaries. Begin today moving in excellence.

Get Rid of Negativity

In order to live a life of excellence you must remove the negativity. Negativity clouds your focus and will eventually wear you down. Raise the rent on negativity and kick it out of your life. There are two main highways that negativity uses to access our lives: it comes either through our own "stink'n think'n" or through relationships.

We must first win the battle between our own two ears and eliminate any negative thought cycles. We must learn to develop a positive self-image by learning from our defeats, focusing on our victories, and moving forward. There will always be negativity in life, but it does not have to abide in you. Your focus is extremely important. What you focus on, you empower. Do not magnify and empower negativity by giving it your attention. Learn to focus on the positive and verbalize those things through positive self-talk.

There is power in the tongue. What you speak is extremely important. You cannot live a life of excellence if you are constantly concentrating on and verbalizing defeat. The word in your mouth will always become a work in your hand. Your words can develop into a positive or negative work, depending on what you speak. I love what the Bible says in James 3:4 where we read: "Or take ships as an example. Although they are so large and are driven by strong winds, they are steered by a very small rudder wherever the pilot wants to go." Our tongue is a small muscle, but it can control our entire life.

If you think and speak defeat and despair, you will live defeat and despair. Likewise, if you think and speak positivity and prosperity, you will reap those benefits. So just remember, words are like seeds being planted in the ground—they will produce a harvest.

Negativity also comes through other people. Everyone knows someone who always seems to have something negative to say, someone who is critical and judgmental of everything and everybody. Always remember that people too weak to follow through on their own vision and goal will always find a way to criticize and discourage yours. Zig Ziglar put it this way: "The only taste of success that some people ever get is when they take a bite out of you."

Some people need drama like they need oxygen. Do not tolerate the company of people who have constant chaos in their life. While there are exceptions, most people with chaotic lives are not simply victims of uncontrollable circumstances. The chaos dwells in them. In life we have to deal with enough negativity without inviting it in on ourselves, so know your circle! Make absolutely sure that everyone in your boat is holding a paddle and not a drill. Oftentimes, some of the very people who we think are there to help us paddle are actually trying to sink us.

Other times, some of the people closest to us may mean well, but they may have a negative opinion or outlook of our vision and goal. In those cases we have to adjust our filter. You have to have the discernment and courage to be able to listen, but also to know when you need to continue to move forward.

Get Moving

It's been said that the greatest day in a person's life is not the day they are born, but the day they find out why. Once you get a vision, and you begin to move in excellence toward your vision, and you have removed the negativity, then it is time to get moving! Start today. Never look back, and never give up. There will be obstacles thrown in your path along the way, but always remember that forward movement turns obstacles into opportunities. Too many people give up, not realizing that they are on the cusp of breakthrough. Often when the battle is strongest, the victory is closest. George Barna said, "Vision without perseverance is like an interesting chapter in an unfinished book." We must persist in our purpose.

We persist by eliminating doubt. A double-minded man is unstable in all his ways. You must pick a horse and ride it. You cannot do everything, and you cannot be all things to all people. Find what you are good at and make it excellent! I have witnessed so many people in life who constantly waver in their opinions. They can't seem to make a decision and stick to it to save their life. Relationally, spiritually, vocationally, they are all over the map.

You can spend your life trying to be a jack-of-all-trades and know a little about a lot, but it will not get you very far. You will end up so stretched out and overextended that you are no good to anyone. When you don't pick an area of focus, you end up frustrated and burnt out before you even get started, straining relationships and your home life. You cannot build anything of lasting significance in life without a team. No man is an island to himself, and an unpredictable leader will produce tentative followers. Excellence requires stability, persistency and consistency.

The Excellence Effect in Everyday Life

I want to end by telling you a story about my life, a story that I believe brings the message of the Excellence Effect full circle. I come from a great family. My siblings and I grew up in a loving home with great parents, and we were raised wonderfully. We were not wealthy, but my parents worked hard to provide for us to the very best of their ability, often making large sacrifices for our financial well-being and happiness.

It was the late '80s and my parents had finally arrived at a place where they were able to build our family's first home. They bought two acres of land out in the country and built a 1,400-square-foot home. That two-acre plot of land was next to a fence that enclosed a farm pasture that bordered our property. After living there awhile, I came to befriend a horse that stayed in that pasture. I loved animals and had a particular affection towards horses. After living in the city in a small apartment it had become a dream of my family to one day have our own farm animals, particularly a horse.

The thing about the late '80s is that it was a tough financial climate. Interest was high and for a middle-class family we were just happy to be out of the city and able to purchase the land and build the home. Too young to understand, I didn't quite realize at my young age what a massive investment an animal of that size was. I didn't understand that you couldn't just buy a horse and that would be the end of it, that they ate tremendous amounts of food, needed a lot of fence and a barn, among many other things. My parents were wise and didn't go into debt to gratify an immediate want but they kept the dream alive and encouraged us kids to as well.

I came to learn that the horse next door had a name, Vandel, and Vandel was not just any horse. He was a quarter horse, and not just any quarter horse, but a direct descendent of a famous bloodline for that breed. He was beautiful; he was bay in color with four white stockings and a white star in the center of his forehead. I would come home from school in the afternoon and take a carrot or an apple or whatever I could nab from the kitchen and head out to the fence to talk to Vandel and share an afternoon snack. We became buddies, and even though I knew we could never afford a horse like Vandel, I had a vision to one day be able to own and ride one just like him.

After some time had passed, one Saturday morning my dad woke me up and told me to get ready, that we were going to the hardware store. At the hardware store I watched as several men loaded bags of concrete mix and several posts into the back of the truck. On the ride home I questioned my dad about what the project for the day was going to be, and he told me that we were going home to begin work on a fence. You cannot imagine the excitement! As kids often do I expected we would build the fence on Saturday and have a horse by Sunday. Of course, that was not the case.

The funds were still not there for a horse but my dad made a decision that morning: He decided that, even though we couldn't write a check, blink our eyes, and do it all at once, we were going to step out. He decided that, even though we may not have a lot and we may not be able to do it all immediately, we could start—we could begin. We were only able to buy a few posts that day but we bought what we could afford. We went home and my dad took a pair of post hole diggers and began digging the holes for the fence posts we had purchased, and by the end of that Saturday we had a great start to a long-held family dream and vision.

Every Saturday from then forward we would buy as many posts as we could afford, some weeks we bought a lot and some weeks we bought a few, but we never gave up. We did the very best with what we had! We had decided that we could sit around and wait forever for circumstances and finances to get "just right," or we could begin with what we had, go as far as we could see that Saturday, and then plan and prepare for the next week. Every weekend we would accomplish more and more.

Not long after starting the fence project we were given a saddle and a rope. My dad would fasten the saddle to the few sections of fence that were finished and my brother and I would put on our western shirt, boots and cowboy hat and sit on that saddle for hours, pretending that it was our horse. I am sure that we looked a little off-center to a lot of people as they drove by our property and saw us spurring a fence and yelling "giddy up," but we didn't care—we were speaking our dream.

An awesome thing happened in our lives as we began to work hard and, with persistence, consistently move toward our dream. People began to take notice. Friends of my parents would ride by and see the work, stop, and ask what we were building—and some began to get out and help. This grew over time until on Saturdays more and more people were showing up—people who were skilled in construction, people who had the tools to do the job more efficiently. We no longer had to dig holes by hand because a man loaned us his tractor with a large auger bit. We no longer had to hammer nails by hand because a friend brought an air-compressed nail gun.

Before we knew it, the fence project was complete and we moved right into building a barn. We had ten or twelve people showing up most Saturdays. My mother would cook large lunches to feed everyone as they worked. It was an exciting time. Hardware store owners were hearing about the project through some of the workers and would donate windows and doors that they had at their store. It was amazing! In just a few short months not only did we have a fence but we had a nice barn with four horse stalls, a tack and feed room, and a hay loft! To just ride by you would have thought we were real-life ranchers!

Shortly after the barn was built, I came home from school one day and my parents told me that the day had come! We were finally getting a horse, as a matter of fact we already had the horse! I ran through the door across the backyard and jumped the fence, made a sharp right turn into the alleyway of the barn and there the horse stood! It was magnificent! Bay in color—just like I wanted—four white stockings, and a white star in the center of his forehead, and then it hit me. This horse looked very familiar. It was Vandel! I couldn't believe it. By this time my parents had rounded the corner with big smiles on their faces. They explained that the neighbor had made Vandel available to us at a great price that they were able to afford. I was ecstatic! Not only did we now have a horse, but we had the very one that I had spent every afternoon with, never thinking we would ever be able to own.

After purchasing Vandel we were given another horse as a gift, so now my dad had a horse of his own and we were able to ride together. We later purchased another, and another, which led to buying more property and building a bigger barn, until eventually we had 50 acres, 12 horses, and kept an average of 60 head of cattle. Many of the men who worked on the fence and barn project with us also bought horses, and we would all take weekend trips riding. We had a tremendous amount of fun during those years.

Living this story as an adolescent taught me a lot about life. You and I have to take a step. We have to begin to move on our dreams and visions. We can either take a step forward or sit around forever and complain about the resources, training, or knowledge that we don't have. When my parents made the decision to begin to do the very best with what they had, things began to happen for us. We did not have all the pieces, we simply stepped out in faith and began to consistently persist in our purpose.

You may feel as if the vision for your life is a million miles away, but let me encourage you today that it is closer than you think—it is in your reach! I didn't know if we would ever be able to afford a nice horse, but little did I know that every day when I walked over to the fence bordering our property, I was petting my horse all along. It seemed a million miles away even though it had actually been placed right next door for me. The vision was there, it was simply waiting on us to make a move.

Many people never get to own their horse, live their dream, or walk in their vision because they never plan and prepare. In the same way that you can't own a horse without somewhere to put him, you can't live your dream without first doing the practical things and building the structure to house it. Many people who want to have the providential have never done the practical. Begin working on you, become a student;

learn, grow, build your character; take a step, and begin to use and do the very best with what you have, and more will come.

As we took a step and began to work on the fence each week using what we had, it began to inspire people. We may have only been able to afford four posts to bury some weeks, but we made sure they were placed properly, that they were level, and that we had done an excellent job. This inspired people and released the power of synergy as friends and family began to catch the vision and join alongside us, bringing resources with them and increasing our efficiency.

We were being fulfilled as they helped us get what we wanted in life, and they were fulfilled because they were able to function in their gifting. Together we were able to accomplish so much more; new relationships were gained and old relationships were strengthened. Through those relationships more resources were released than we ever could have imagined. This inspiration moved through the whole group as many of these people purchased horses themselves. Excellence really is contagious! Zig Ziglar's core message is: "You can have everything in life you want if you will just help enough other people get what they want."
Always remember: Excellence honors God and inspires people. Live and demonstrate a life of excellence by using what you have, where you are, to the very best of your ability—and watch things begin to accelerate for you. You have to start somewhere. You may not have a lot, but make sure that you do the best with what you have and watch it multiply and become more. Persist in your purpose and you will experience a life lived in excellence. ▮

 J. JUSTIN YOUNG *is a motivational speaker, business consultant, and trainer. He is certified and endorsed by Ziglar, Inc. (Ziglar Legacy Certification), and travels the United States and abroad as a keynote speaker for corporate conventions, municipalities, social organizations, churches, and nonprofits. Delivering a core message of excellence and its profound effect on every aspect of life, Justin* also teaches Zig Ziglar's proven workshops on topics such as "Building the Best You," "Building Winning Relationships," and "Goal Setting and Achievement." An aspiring author, his first book,* The Excellence Effect, *is set for release in early 2015. Justin's life mission is to "Impact, Impart, and Empower Leaders to Experience a Life Lived in Excellence."*

Justin Young
jyoung@paramountbenefitsgroup.com